STUDIES IN THE LIFE AND MINISTRY OF THE HISTORICAL JESUS

Raymond A. Martin

UNIVERSITY
PRESS OF
AMERICA

Lanham • New York • London

Copyright© 1995 by
University Press of America,® Inc.
4720 Boston Way
Lanham, Maryland 20706

3 Henrietta Street
London, WC2E 8LU England

Library of Congress Cataloging-in-Publication Data

Martin, Raymond A.
Studies in the life and ministry of the historical Jesus / Raymond
A. Martin.
p. cm.
Includes bibliographical references and indexes.
1. Jesus Christ--Historicity. 2. Jesus Christ--Biography.
3. Bible. N.T. Gospels--Criticism, interpretation, etc.
4. Palestine--Biography.   I. Title.
BT303.2.M385   1994
232.9'08--dc20   94-38389 CIP

ISBN 0-8191-9772-6 (cloth: alk paper)
ISBN 0-8191-9773-4 (pbk.: alk paper)

"The central feature of Synoptic research must continue to be the attempt to get back to Jesus himself."

M. Hengel

"One is looking for a hypothesis which explains more (not everything), which gives a good account (not the only one) of what happened, which fits Jesus realistically into his environment, and which has in view cause and effect."

E. P. Sanders

For Alice
"Many women have done excellently,
But you surpass them all."
Proverbs 31:39

and for our children: Bill, Barb, Mary, Tim,
and their children and their children's children

"Children are a heritage from the Lord,
Happy are they who have their
quiver full of them."
Psalm 127:5

Contents

Preface

In the past decade there has been a resurgence of studies of the historical Jesus. E. P. Sanders has recently written: "The dominant view today seems to be that we can know pretty well what Jesus was out to accomplish, that we can know a lot about what he said, and that those two things make sense within the world of first-century Judaism."[1] Others have expressed similar confidence.[2]

This study seeks to join in that revival. Often it is made to appear that Jesus sets out with a fairly clear understanding of what he is to do, and maintains that basic understanding until his death. It seems to me, however, that the traditions preserved in the Gospel accounts reveal a man who in early manhood becomes aware that God has a special task for him to do and who then struggles to understand both what that task is and how it is to be carried out. In that process Jesus' own thinking appears to undergo modification and development. It is this development that these studies seek to trace.

Jesus is the central figure in Christianity and a significant figure for many other people as well. In such an historical study it is, perhaps, appropriate to indicate at the outset my own relationship to Jesus Christ. I accept the witness of the New Testament and the Church down the ages that Jesus is both truly and fully God and also truly and fully human. While this faith-stance over against Jesus could, indeed often has, led people to seek in the Gospel accounts proof of Jesus' divinity, it need not lead to that. The Scriptures themselves, more than few times, indicate that Jesus is a limited human being, living his life as any human being must, in trust and uncertainty. Paul seeks to express this in Philippians 2:4ff. where (quoting an early Christian hymn) he says that the pre-existent One "emptied himself." While the full meaning of that concept may never be accurately understood, my own position is

ix

that this means: Jesus during his human existence (from conception through his resurrection by the Father) *is unaware of and has no independent use of any of his divine nature or powers.* Whatever insights he has and whatever miracles he does, he does by the same power that any human being trusting God might do. Thus the Bible presents him as saying about his miracles, for example, that he does them by the power of the Holy Spirit (Mark 3:22-30) and that whoever believes in him will be able to do the same works that Jesus does, and even greater ones *"because,"* he says, *"I go to the Father"* (John 14:12).

It is with this understanding of the *humanness* of Jesus that this study will consider the traditions found in the Gospel accounts—neither seeking to discover evidence for nor to prove or disprove the deity of Jesus; rather seeking to follow Jesus' very human struggles to understand and live out the Father's will for him. In other words this is an historical study of an historical human being who was a Jew living in Palestine in the first century C.E. and who is to be understood in the light of that milieu.

Raymond Martin
Wartburg Theological Seminary
Dubuque, Iowa
1994

Introduction

Before proceeding to a reconstruction of Jesus' life and thought it is appropriate to consider again the methodology to be followed. None of the extant writings concerning Jesus is contemporaneous with his lifetime. As far as can be determined all of them have been written by committed followers of the crucified and risen Jesus and these traditions are overlaid to a greater or lesser extent with the theological concerns and literary structures of their authors.[3] Over the years (particularly since the middle of the 20th century) criteria have been developed to further the task of getting behind these later literary structures and interpretations in order to see more clearly Jesus in his own times in Palestine during the first half of the first century C.E.

While the lists of criteria used by scholars vary somewhat[4], there is general agreement on the basic importance of five of them.[5] In the pages that follow these five criteria will generally be used to isolate where a writer is using traditional material, with concentration on those traditions which have been handed on in the Aramaic-speaking Christian community in the first half of the first century C.E.[6] Then, as far as possible, it will seek to uncover those traditions which reveal the life and thought of Jesus himself, particularly as these traditions relate to his understanding of his role in God's plans and the way he feels he should carry out that role.

The earliest[7], and for many scholars the most important, criterion is what has come to most commonly be called *"the criterion of dissimilarity."*[8] This criterion has considerable value in isolating those features in which Jesus differs from both his Jewish environment and the earliest Christian community; i.e., his uniqueness. The disadvantage, however, as has been frequently noted, is that used alone and wrongly it results in caricature, since it cannot recover the

1

overwhelming similarity between Jesus and the Jewish environment in which he grew up, lived and worked. Nor does it reveal the continuity which to some degree Jesus had with the earliest Christian community.[9] This criterion will, however, be very useful in the case of those Aramaic traditions where Jesus is seen to be in disagreement with ideas held by the early Palestinian Aramaic-speaking Church.

The next criterion, which Schillebeeckx calls *"the criterion of the context, whether linguistic or cultural-cum-geographical,"*[10] needs more detailed discussion. Schillebeeckx considers this criterion to be invalid, since the early Church as well as Jesus spoke Aramaic and had Palestine as their milieu.[11] It has also been frequently pointed out that there is difficulty in finding agreed upon criteria of Aramaic traditions, particularly in light of the common use of the LXX and the influence (conscious or unconscious) it may have had on the language of the writers.[12] Further, there were also Greek-speaking early Christians so that Greek traditions may also go back to the earliest period.[13] Because of such difficulties there has generally been a strong tendency to disregard especially the linguistic aspect of this criterion. Such disuse, however, deserves reconsideration. Whatever decision is made about this criterion, it, like each of the other criteria, cannot be used alone but rather in combination with the others.

Two primary difficulties have been noted concerning the occurrence of Semitic linguistic features in a document: Are these features the result a) of a person having learned Greek in a bi-lingual environment, so that the Semitic features are the *unconscious* result of that bilingual environment[14] or b) the *deliberate* adoption of Semitic features by a skilled writer who seeks thereby to impart Palestinian Hebrew/Aramaic coloring to his narration? Sparks has pressed this second point particularly.[15] He writes concerning Luke's so-called "Septaugintalisms":

> They are, if the phrase may be excused, nothing less than 'pieces of literary scenery,' deliberately devised and cunningly conceived to provide the right background for the action... Yet not all parts of Luke-Acts are equally Septuagintal. This is due, I suggest, to St. Luke's historical as well as to his dramatic sense... The background of the ministry was historically Palestinian, and so also was the background of the primitive Church; so St. Luke selects for both a consciously Semitic, and because he was a Gentile, writing for Gentiles, a necessarily almost entirely Septuagintal style.[16]

In this judgment he has been followed, e.g., by Conzelmann,[17] Haenchen,[18] Fitzmyer (to a degree)[19] and others.

However, the *distribution* of the evidence of Semitic influence as determined by syntax criticism[20] in the Synoptics and Acts shows that both of the above explanations are unlikely. In detailed studies of these 17 criteria of translation Greek in the Synoptic Gospels it was found that they do not occur with Semitic frequencies consistently in any of them, but rather are *erratically* distributed so that some stories and some statements appear as translation Greek while others correspond with original Greek style. This erratic distribution is difficult to understand if they are the result of a writer's *natural style* which has been influenced by his bilingualism or subconsciously by his acquaintance with the Septaugint.[21]

The more commonly held view, namely Luke's *skillful and deliberate* imitation of LXX style, is not satisfactory either. The data from Luke-Acts is particularly instructive here.[22]

First of all, consider the book of Acts. The second half (Acts 15:36 - 28:31) is *consistently* like the original Greek control documents studied.[23] This is the writer's natural style and is a good "control" for studying Luke's language elsewhere.[24] The first half (Acts 1:1 - 15:35), however, is erratic with respect to occurrence of these 17 criteria—22 of some 58 units having Semitic frequencies characteristic of translation Greek.[25]

One cannot help but ask, if Luke *deliberately* introduced a LXX-like style in these stories from the first half of Acts as being appropriate to a Palestinian setting, as Sparks and others posit, why does he do so *only in some* stories (some of which have a Palestinian setting and some of which do not have a Palestinian setting)? And why does he not adopt this style in the many other places where the Palestinian background is clear and obvious? A few examples will be found instructive.[26] Why should Luke choose to use a Semitic style for narrating Paul's experiences and the healing of a man crippled from birth outside of Palestine at Lystra *in Asia Minor* (Acts 14:8-20), but use his natural non-Semitic style to describe Peter and John's *similar experience with a man lame from birth in Jerusalem* (Acts 3:1-10)? Or why deliberately adopt a Semitic style to narrate the arrest, imprisonment and trial of Peter and other apostles in Jerusalem in Acts 5:17-32, but not use it for the arrest, imprisonment and trial of Peter and John in Jerusalem in the previous chapter (Acts 4:5-22)? Or why should Luke's narration of

Peter's vision and his visit to Cornelius be told in his natural, non-Semitic style (Acts 10:1-48), but Peter's retelling of it in Acts 11:5-17 be highly Semitized as indicated by these 17 syntactical features? Finally, why would the writer use a very Semitic style for Paul's sermon in Antioch of Asia Minor (Acts 13:16b-41), but employ his natural, non-Semitic style for Paul's speech before the mob in Jerusalem, which Luke specifically says was delivered in Aramaic (Acts 22:2-21)? There, if anywhere, he surely ought to seek to give Semitic coloring to the Greek! It is most probable, rather, that when these 17 syntactical criteria of syntax criticism appear with Semitic frequencies in Lukan writings they are to be seen as evidence that Semitic traditional materials are being used.

But more. When Luke's *Gospel* is analyzed by means of these 17 criteria the same erratic distribution occurs.[27] Why is not the entire *Gospel* written in such deliberately Semitized Greek since the Gospel material is entirely set within a Palestinian environment? And why, as a study of his use of Markan material shows, does Luke tend generally to *lessen* the Semitic style of Mark (as determined by these 17 criteria), as he does nearly 3/4 of the time? Since all of Mark's material has a Palestinian setting, it is difficult to understand why Luke would make Markan material he uses less rather than more Semitic.[28] Why is some of Luke's Q material Semitic and some not? And why is nearly 1/3 of Luke's special material Semitic?—all of Q and all of Luke's special material have a Palestinian setting. How improbable that this situation should be Luke's deliberate and skillful adopting of a Semitic Greek style to provide a more appropriate language for a Palestinian setting.

It becomes even more improbable, however, when it is seen that such *erratic Semitic style with respect to these 17 syntactical features appears in both Mark and Matthew!*[29] Is it to be assumed that they, like Luke, are so skilled as to be able consciously to imitate the style of the Greek of the Old Testament so as to give appropriate coloring to their Gospels? And, if so, why do they, like Luke, also do it only in some stories and sayings and not others? One final interesting example. Why should Mark adopt a very Semitic style for his narration of the feeding of the 4000 (Mark 8:1-10) and a very *non*-Semitic style for his narration of the feeding of the 5000 (Mark 6:30-44)? Or why should Matthew (Matt. 15:32-39) change Mark's narration of the feeding of the 4000 and eliminate much of this Semitic style, which Matthew uses elsewhere both in his Q material and (at times) in his special material?

Surely the most probable explanation for this inconsistency is that Semitic sources/traditions are being used.[30]

In the pages that follow, then, where these 17 syntactical criteria show up with Semitic frequencies in Synoptic Gospel material this will be taken to indicate traditional material being used which goes back to a Palestinian Aramaic-speaking milieu of the Church and possibly also to Jesus.

The situation concerning John's Gospel is different. The detailed analysis of that Gospel by these 17 criteria shows it, surprisingly, to be highly Semitized, much more so than any of the Synoptics.[31] This would seem to indicate that the bulk of that Gospel goes back to at least the Aramaic stages (1 and 2) as posited by Brown[32] and some of it may also go back to traditions from Jesus' lifetime.

A third criterion frequently used to recover authentic Jesus material is the criterion of multiple attestation.[33] It is applied in two ways: referring 1) to attestation of material which occurs in two or more independent sources; and 2) to material occurring in different literary genre (forms). A few comments about both of these. The main generally-agreed-upon *independent* sources are Mark; Q; Lukan special material; Matthean special material; the Coptic Gospel of Thomas; John's Gospel. If a story or saying occurs in 2 or more of these, it obviously has its roots very early in the tradition. Some find this to be the most useful criteria.[34] The issue is, of course, whether these traditions are independent of each other. This has been debated especially both with respect to the Gospel of Thomas[35] and also the Gospel of John. For purposes of this study both are considered to contain independent traditions.[36] There has also been much debate whether Q ever existed and whether Matthew rather than Mark is the independent Gospel used by the others. Fitzmyer has convincingly demonstrated once again the priority of Mark and the use by Matthew and Luke of the source designated as Q.[37] It may be noted that the syntax criticism study of the Synoptics supports this conclusion.[38]

Concerning multiple attestation by a variety of literary forms Schillebeeckx writes: "The criterion carries more weight where the same sort of content is to be found in diverse forms."[39] McArthur, however, prefers multiple attestation by independent sources.[40] The criterion of variety of forms is significant for material whether found in a single source or in a number of the independent sources.

Another frequently used criterion is *consistency*[41]—usually understood to designate a tradition which is consistent with critically assured authentic material (which has been found to be authentic by other criteria).[42]   Schillebeeckx prefers using this criterion to show consistency with the *total picture of Jesus' life,* "which as a historical end-result gradually arises out of the detailed analysis and then in turn leads to further analysis in detail."[43]

The final criterion generally in use is, in Schillebeeckx's wording, *"The criterion of rejection of Jesus' message and praxis: his execution."*[44] According to this criterion that which would cause offense to Jewish and Roman authorities and might lead to Jesus' execution by them has a good probability of authenticity.[45]   This is, in one sense, similar to the preceding criterion of consistency: that which is consistent with the undoubted execution of Jesus by both Jewish and Roman authorities.

As has been frequently noted[46] these criteria and others must be used together. No one of them is sufficient by itself. Further, at best, only probability not absolute certainty, concerning the authenticity of Jesus material can be attained due to the limitations imposed by the nature and extent of the extant sources.[47]

This study is structured in keeping with fairly certain stages of Jesus' life[48] as preserved in the traditions, particularly those which appear to have had special significance for Jesus as he seeks to understand his role in God's plans.

1. Jesus' Birth and Early Years
2. Baptism by John the Baptist
3. From Baptism to the Imprisonment of John
4. From John's Imprisonment to John's Death
5. Jesus' Final Trip to Jerusalem.

In the Epilogue the question will be addressed as to what it was that caused Jesus' disciples (in the broad sense of the term) to unite in a community which confesses Jesus to be God's Messiah and which undertakes a mission to proclaim Jesus' Messiahship to both Jew and Gentile? It is in that connection that the traditions of Jesus' resurrection will be studied.

Chapter 1

Jesus' Birth and Early Years

While little is said about this period of Jesus' life in the canonical Gospels, the little there is has the marks of earlier traditions which are being used by Matthew and Luke. These traditions reveal the milieu in which Jesus was born, grew up and developed.

The Birth of Jesus

While it is not possible to give the exact year of Jesus' birth, it is quite clear that it occurred before the death of Herod the Great. This is doubly attested (Matt 2:1,22; Luke 1:5-2:6).[49] Herod's death occurred in 4 B.C.E. There are a number of events noted by Josephus which establish this date. First of all, Josephus recounts that there was a lunar eclipse shortly before the death of Herod and that a Passover followed soon thereafter (*Ant.* XVII. vi, 4; viii, 1; ix, 3). Such a lunar eclipse occurred March 12/13 of 4 B.C.E. which was about a month before Passover of that year.[50]

Another line of evidence from Josephus leads to the same date. Josephus dates the battle of Actium in the 7th year of Herod (*Ant.*XV. v. 2) which is 31 B.C.E. Josephus uses the inclusive method of dating and is calculating this date in Herod's reign from the beginning of his *de facto* ruling in 37 B.C.E. Since Herod died in the 34th year of his reign, his death occurred in the year 4 B.C.E.[51]

There is yet another line of evidence (also from Josephus). Archelaus was appointed by Herod's will as ruler over Judea and Samaria. This was confirmed by Rome not long after Herod's death. Since Archelaus was deposed in 6 C.E. by Rome in the 9th year of his reign, this means Archelaus began his ruling in 4 B.C.E.[52] There is no way to determine how long before the death of Herod Jesus was born. Most modern datings put it some two years earlier (7-5 B.C.E.) apparently based on the remark in Matt. 2:16 that Herod "killed all the male children in Bethlehem and in all that region who were two years old and under." While this kind of act conforms well with Herod's practices in the last years of his life, it may be nothing more than an evidence of the midrashic style of these chapters in Matthew.

The canonical sources for information about the birth and earliest years of Jesus are the so-called "infancy stories" in Matt. 1; 2 and Luke 1; 2. While in some ways they are similar and do, as will be pointed out below, contain a common core of early traditions about Jesus' birth, they both have clear marks of literary composition. The question needs, then, to be asked to what extent, if any, do the accounts themselves go back to pre-Matthean or pre-Lukan sources?

Generally in the case of Matthew's Gospel scholars have found little or no evidence of sources being used in these two chapters, but rather see them as the writer's own composition. The style has been called "midrashic" but this is to be understood in a loose "story-telling" sense.[53] If the Matthean account is somehow related to earlier sources, these would have been most immediately Greek sources according to the evidence of syntax criticism. An analysis of Matt. 1 and 2 by this methodology shows that these are among the least Semitic of all of Matthew's special material, with only the small section 1:22, 24, 25 somewhat approaching clear translation Greek frequencies.[54]

The situation is much different with the Lukan account.[55] There is nearly universal agreement that much of Luke 1 and 2 are very Semitic, with the only debate being concerned with the cause of this Semitic style.[56] There have been three types of explanations for this highly Semitic style of the Lukan infancy narratives: 1) Luke's natural Semitized style[57]; 2) Luke's deliberately chosen Septuagintal style[58]; 3) evidence of Luke's using Semitic sources.[59] That this last explanation is most probable has been demonstrated in the Introduction (*supra*, pp. 2ff.) and those arguments need not be repeated here. It is in place to discuss briefly what is meant by the term "source." It is not used in its narrowest sense of an extensive continuous narrative. Rather it designates a block of material which goes back to either an oral or written earlier tradition, in this case in either Aramaic or Hebrew.[60] It need not be extensive; it may at times refer to a smaller unit of tradition or a previous grouping of material (such as, for example, a collection of miracle stories, parables, sayings, etc.). It may also be a short collection of events (such as the proposed sequence behind Mark chapter 6 and chapter 8 and the similar grouping in John 6).[61] For the purposes of this study the important point is that in such Semitic blocks of material in the Gospels evidence of earlier Semitic traditions is recognizable, traditions which go back to the Palestinian, Aramaic milieu, whether that of the Palestinian Aramaic-speaking Church or that of Jesus, his family and of those who followed him during his lifetime.[62]

It is significant then that each of the smaller units in Luke 1:5-80 individually and as a group fall deeply into the area of translation Greek as calculated by syntax criticism,[63] as well as some of the more erratic data of Luke 2:1-52.[64] Whatever the decision about whether to think of this material as going back to 'sources' or 'traditions', and whether these were oral or written, syntax criticism confirms the judgment of numerous scholars[65] that the material here has a Palestinian, Semitic-language milieu.

Also whether the tradition that Luke was the writer of the Gospel and of Acts is correct or not does not make a great deal of difference.[66] It is possible for someone who knows Greek very well also to have facility in Aramaic,[67] and also Hebrew. What an author could or could not do cannot be decided in the abstract, particularly when little or nothing is known about him. It has been suggested that either the author himself translated these Semitic sources or they came to him already translated into Greek.[68] In any case the transmission of these Palestinian traditions of Jesus' early life could well have been via the family of Jesus since some of them at least soon after the resurrection became Jesus' followers and eventually took over the leadership of the Palestinian Church.[69] There is no way to determine the role of Mary in this process, but it should not be surprising if she were also involved.[70]

Both Brown[71] and Fitzmyer[72] note a large number of details shared between the independent infancy narratives of Matthew and Luke. Four items of their longer quite similar listings are particularly significant:
1. Jesus' birth before the death of Herod the Great;
2. Jesus' birth in Bethlehem;
3. Jesus' early years in Nazareth of Galilee;
4. Jesus' non-normal parentage.

These four items are doubly-attested and as Fitzmyer notes "must be regarded as derived from an earlier tradition. Opinions will vary as to the historical value of such traditional details, but I tend to regard them as the historical nucleus of what the evangelists worked with."[73]

Luke's narration has an additional feature—the Levitic relatives of Mary and a form of the genealogy of Jesus which contains, as some of his nearest ancestors, Levitic names. While this will be discussed a bit later when the genealogies are considered, it is important to note that this recollection of the Levitic ancestry of Jesus is probably authentic since a) it does not fit very well with the early Church's proclamation of Jesus as the Davidic Messiah (criterion of dissimilarity) and b) finds confirmation in later Church traditions concerning Jesus' brother James, who is spoken of as a priest carrying out high priestly functions.[74]

Jesus' Ancestry

There are two genealogical lists of Jesus' ancestors: Matthew 1:1-17 and Luke 3:23-38. These listings do not agree with one another.[75] Fitzmyer has summarized the situation succinctly:

> The main problem in the interpretation of the Lucan genealogy arises from the comparison of it with the Matthean (1:1-17), which differs notably. The two lists agree in tracing Jesus' pedigree through Joseph in mentioning Zerubbabel and Shealtiel in the post exilic period (Luke 3:27; Matt. 1:12) and in tracing part of the pedigree in the monarchic period and earlier from Abraham to Hezron (Luke 3:33-35; Matt. 1:2-3) and from Amminadab to David (Luke 3:31-33; Matt. 1:3-6). But apart from that they go their own ways.[76]

He then points out "the main differences;" some of the most important ones he lists are:[77]

1. Luke adds the ancestors of Abraham back to Adam.
2. Luke has many more names in the periods covered by the two genealogies than Matthew's list has.
3. In the post-exilic section after Zerubbabel none of Luke's 18 ancestors are the same as Matthew's 9!
4. Very significantly Luke lists Jesus' grandfather as Heli (=Eli)[78] (3:23) whereas Matthew has Jacob (1:16).

It should also be noted that a surprisingly large number of names in Luke's genealogy (in contrast to Matthew's) are clearly priestly names: e.g. Levi (3:24, 29), Mattathias (3:25, 26), Heli (Eli) (3:23).[79]

How is the existence of two such radically different genealogical lists for Jesus' ancestry to be understood? It is generally conceded that while both lists certainly are molded and shaped by the Evangelists to serve their distinctive purposes, both of them seem to be drawing upon earlier traditional listings. Concerning Matthew Brown writes: "Either Matthew has created the genealogy himself, or, more probably, he has added the names of Joseph and Jesus to an existing genealogy which Matthew joined to a pre-Davidic era list resembling those in Ruth 4:18-22 and 1 Chr. 2:1-15."[80] Similarly concerning Luke's list Fitzmyer writes:

> It is obvious that Luke could have consulted his Greek OT in the passages cited above and constructed the list accordingly, either digging out the others from literature unknown to us or filling them in himself. Yet modern commentators (e.g. W. Grundmann, *Evangelium nach Lukas*, 111; H. Schurmann, *Lukasevangelium*, 203; G. Schneider, *Evangelium nach Lukas*, 94) prefer to think that Luke has made use of a previously existing genealogy. This is in my opinion more likely.[81]

The simplest solution to this problem is to see Matthew's listing as presenting the Davidic genealogy of Jesus through his step-father Joseph, and the Levitic segment of Luke's listing reflecting the priestly lineage of Mary's family, of which Luke is clearly aware and preserves in the Baptist traditions he uses concerning Mary's relatives in Judea in chapter one.

While this solution had been proposed already in the 15th century and possibly even much earlier,[82] scholars have generally rejected it.[83] Brown objects to this solution because 1) Jewish genealogy does not normally trace lineage through the mother; 2) Luke intends to gives *Davidic* descent and "we really do not know that Mary was a Davidid."[84] Fitzmyer also rejects it: "Though tradition has at times thought of Mary's Davidic descent, there is no basis for this in the NT; and Luke has traced the genealogy of Jesus specifically through Joseph."[85] Marshall also takes objection to this because of the intended Davidic lineage of the Lukan genealogy.[86]

There is no doubt that the Lukan genealogy, like the Matthean, traces Jesus' lineage through Joseph back to David; however, it appears the tradition Luke took over preserves a recollection of *Mary's priestly descent*; and either that earlier form of the tradition or Luke himself has conformed this priestly lineage to the Joseph/Davidic line which was the dominant early Christian concern. It may be noted that the priests, more than any other group in this period, had a need to keep genealogical records; so the occurrence of such a listing in a family with priestly lineage would not be completely out of the question.[87] The first chapter of Luke's Gospel in which Mary's priestly relatives are noted is, by the analysis of syntax criticism,[88] among the most Semitic of Luke's special material, indicating that Mary's priestly lineage is a pre-Lukan Palestinian tradition. While it is correct, as Brown indicates, that the Lukan list has little more claim than Matthew's to be factual,[89] it does seem evident that there was a strong priestly tradition in the lineage of Mary and consequently also in the lineage of her son and this is what Luke preserves.[90]

Jesus' Birthplace

As noted *supra* (p. 9) Jesus' birth in Bethlehem and his subsequent early years in Nazareth are a doubly attested common tradition of Matthew and Luke. They disagree, it appears, radically as to *how* this shift of location comes about.

Luke's traditions clearly make Nazareth Mary's home town and the move to Bethlehem comes in the final stages of her pregnancy because of a census requirement. All the data available to date indicates no such census under Quirinius took place during the reign of Herod the Great[91] and thus this appears to be a literary construction of Luke.

Matthew's account makes no mention of Mary's hometown and describes the birth in Bethlehem as though she and Joseph live there. Especially two details in Matthew's account suggest this was their permanent home: 1) the Magi find Mary and Jesus in a "house" (*oikian*) (2:11); and 2) Herod kills all children two years old and under, as though Jesus might already have reached the age of two (2:16). As noted early Matthew's account clearly contains midrashic elements and thus there can be little certainty about Herod's activities in this connection.[92]

Matthew's use of the word "house" in 2:11 and Luke's *kataluma* (2:7) (incorrectly translated traditionally as "inn") most likely refer to the same thing. The word *kataluma* is a late Greek word used in the papyri for lodgings or quarters for troops. It has a wide range of meanings in the Septuagint including temporary lodgings of visitors to the temple (1 Chron. 28:12) or God's presence in the temple (2 Kings

7:6); a temporary resting place on a journey (Jer. 14:8); a den of a lion [Jer. 32(25):38], etc. In the New Testament it occurs only 2 times outside Luke's birth story—both in the account of the last supper (Luke 22:11 and Mark 14:14). In these cases the reference is to the *guest room of a house.* Luke is aware of and uses the normal Greek word for a commercial lodging place, an inn *pandoxeian,* in 10:34 the story of the "Good Samaritan." Marshall is certainly correct that, as far as New Testament and specifically Lukan usage is concerned, *kataluma* of Luke 2:7 "refers to a room, rather than to an inn..., and to a room in a private house rather than to a room in an inn."[93]

The term Luke uses for the place in which the infant Jesus was placed is *phatnē.* This word normally means the place in which the feed for animals was put, i.e., 'crib' or 'manger'. Hengel indicates that at times, both in the papyri and the Septuagint, *phatnē* has the more general meaning 'stall' for animals. He writes *re* Septuagint usage: "'crib' or 'stall' is possible at Is. 1:3; Prov. 14:4, but the latter [stall] is likely only at 2 Ch. 32:28... The few or late ref. to 'stalls' in the OT show that apart from royal stables these were relatively uncommon in Palestine, *since men and animals often lived in the same dwelling* [italics added]."[94]

The account of Jesus' birth in both Luke and Matthew are characterized by evidence of divine activity and supernatural events. This emphasis fits with their interest in presenting Jesus as Messiah and Savior.[95] It may be that in this way the very natural and human aspects of Mary's pre-nuptial pregnancy are no longer evident.

While what follows is certainly only speculation, it is speculation stimulated by the correspondence of these two independent accounts with reference to two points: 1) the family moves from Bethlehem to Nazareth and 2) the birth occurs in a house in Bethlehem.

It is probable that the tradition preserved in Luke that Mary and Joseph originally lived in Nazareth before marriage is correct. The fact that Matthew has them go there from Bethlehem after the birth would fit with this. The census of Quirinius in Luke and the fear about Archelaus in Matthew may be the writers' ways of dealing with the two elements in the tradition which came to them, namely the association of Jesus with both Bethlehem and Nazareth in his earliest years.

The pre-nuptial pregnancy of Mary could only raise great problems for her and for her husband-to-be Joseph (still reflected in the Matthean traditions—cf. 1:19). No one (and particularly those in her family) could be expected to give credence to her claim of a supernatural conception. She may well have gone to visit her aunt in Judea when the reality of her pregnancy became evident to her *before* it would be apparent to others. It may be that she confided in Joseph, who would also be sorely tried to accept her claim. They may have been married in Nazareth in the earliest stages of pregnancy or left Nazareth, separately or together, for Bethlehem to avoid the scandal (which could hardly be avoided in such a small community as Nazareth).

The detail of a house in Bethlehem can well indicate that Joseph (or Mary's family or relatives) had property there. The unavailability of either the house or guest room as recounted in Luke fits well with an unforeseen departure from Galilee and an unexpected arrival in Bethlehem.[96] They may have planned to stay there permanently and later have decided to return to Nazareth as is indicated in both traditions (Luke at least a month: 2:22; Matthew perhaps 2 years: 2:16). The later challenge to Jesus' paternity in John 8:48 ("We are right, aren't we, when we say that you are a Samaritan and have a demon?") may reflect an early tradition of suspicion about the circumstances surrounding Jesus' birth.[97]

The other details in the infancy account of Luke (circumcision, presentation in the Temple, visit to the Temple by the twelve year old Jesus) may be, as Fitzmyer suggests,[98] not recollections of actual happenings in Jesus' early life, but the writer's composition (or redaction of traditions) to show Jesus growing up as a normal Jewish boy with a predilection for spiritual matters.[99]

Finally it may be noted that there is no indication in the traditions that Mary at any time shared with anyone her convictions of the special nature of her son or of his conception (apart from telling Joseph), nor how she herself understood his role in God's plans. The very Semitic traditions in Luke 2:41-52[100] contain the statement that "she 'treasured' (*diatēreō*) all these things in her heart" (2:51; cf. also 2:19, another translation Greek section[101]). It is most probable that Mary's own understanding of her son was a gradual development, climaxed for her, as for others, including Paul, by the resurrection—since a positive relationship of Mary to the adult Jesus is nowhere indicated in the *Synoptic* traditions,[102] but in Acts 1:14 she is listed in the earliest group of believers. The traditions imply that it was in connection with John the Baptist's preaching and Jesus' baptism by John that Jesus himself begins to consider his own future in God's plans for the New Age which John declares is near at hand. This matter will be taken up in the next chapter.

Chapter 2

Baptism by John the Baptist

The appearance, baptizing and message of John the Baptist according to all available traditions evoked expectations for many in Palestine that God was about to bring in the New Age for his people. Not only that, but the Christian traditions universally agree that John's work was of basic importance for the subsequent ministry of Jesus as well.[103] This is somewhat surprising, since the early Church had for a long time a continuing problem with those who considered John more important than Jesus, since he both preceded Jesus and had baptized him. Thus there is little doubt that the traditions about John and his relation to Jesus reflect basically the actual situation.

Four aspects of John's life and ministry as presented in these traditions need to be studied because of the evident significance John has for Jesus' understanding of the approaching reign of God and Jesus' own role with respect to it:

1. John's ministry prior to his baptizing Jesus
2. John's baptism of Jesus and John's understanding of Jesus' role in relation to the approaching New Age
3. The significance of John's imprisonment for Jesus
4. The significance of John's death for Jesus

The sources for a study of John the Baptist are found primarily in Luke's special traditions in chapter 1, Mark, Q, John,[104] Josephus and the Coptic Gospel of Thomas.

John's Ministry Prior to His Baptizing Jesus

Luke 1 which alone tells of the conception and birth of John (1:5-25, 57-80) is some of the most Semitic of Luke's writings, falling deeply into the area of translation Greek as analyzed by syntax criticism.[105] These traditions then go back to a Palestinian Aramaic-speaking milieu.

From these traditions John is seen to be of priestly lineage, from the rural hill country of Judea, and a relative (cousin) of Jesus. Since there is no evident reason why the Palestinian Church would artificially construct such a lineage and a relationship with Jesus, it appears to be an authentic recollection of John's background.

Apart from the above traditions in Luke 1 all other sources take up John's life at later stages, most often beginning with his preaching and baptizing in the wilderness.[106]

Luke alone offers material which purports to date the beginning of the ministry of John the Baptist, placing it "in the fifteenth year of the reign of Tiberius Caesar" (Lk. 3:1).[107] The calculation of a specific year C.E. however, using this datum is complicated by a number of factors. Fitzmyer lists various problematic aspects:[108]

1.   Is the beginning of Tiberius' reign to be dated from the time of his co-regency with Caesar Augustus in either 11 or 12 C.E.? or from the death of Augustus in 14 C.E.?

2.   Did Luke reckon reigns according to the year of accession or the "regnal year?"

3.   Which calendar was he using (Julian, Jewish, Syrian-Macedonian, Egyptian)?

If the beginning of co-regency is the starting point[109] the probable date for John the Baptist's public appearance is ca 26/27 C.E.[110] Most scholars prefer to calculate from the death of Augustus 14 C.E. and this gives the most probable date for the 15th year as 28-29 C.E.[111] Marshall indicates that if the Syrian method of dating is followed, the 15th year would be "one year earlier, i.e., autumn 27 to autumn 28."[112]

There is another chronological notice that relates to this matter also. In John 2:20 the Jews at the time of Jesus' "cleansing" of the Temple remark that the Temple "has been in the process of being built 46 years." Thus it is possible to calculate the date of the utterance, since the date Herod began building the Temple is known from Josephus, i.e. 20/19 B.C.E. (*Ant.*) or 23/22 (*Wars*).[113]

Whether or not this statement is correctly attached to the account of the Temple "cleansing" will be discussed a bit later, but concerning the 46 years there no evident reason why such a strange and specific number should be included in the statement by the writer of John's Gospel unless he had found it in his traditions.[114] Using the above data the range of possible dates when this statement was made would be 24-29 C.E. with the most probable dates being 26-28 C.E.[115] This statement by Jesus would indicate the *terminus ad quem* for the appearance of John, since John preceded Jesus. This corresponds well with the dating of John the Baptist according to Luke 3:1.

John the Baptist is said to be baptising in various places in the traditions. The Synoptics place him in the wilderness of Judea near the Jordan and show crowds from Jerusalem and Judea coming to him there (Mark 1:4f.; Matt. 3:1; Luke 3:3).[116] This would be the area near the northwestern side of the Dead Sea and in the vicinity of the Qumran community. John's Gospel first speaks of him in Bethany beyond Jordan (1:28) which seems to be in Perea, under Herod's jurisdiction,[117] and later at "Aenon near Salem" (3:22) which probably is to be located at modern 'Ainun northeast of Salem in Samaria.[118] It seems most probable, as Flusser suggests,[119] that John the Baptist "moved about quite a lot." It is further probable that his movements reflect to some degree also his interactions with Jesus after he baptized him and with Herod Antipas who eventually arrests him.

The Message of John the Baptist

The general scope of John's ministry is clear from the sources available as Brown indicates:

> As we know from the Synoptics and Josephus (*Ant.* XVIII. v. 2; #118), John the Baptist attracted great crowds by his ministry in the Jordan valley. He had come down from the desert of Judea, those barren hills to the west of the Dead Sea, and with apocalyptic zeal was proclaiming the day of judgment. He administered a baptism of water to those who accepted his message and acknowledged their own sinfulness.[120]

Koester correctly notes that John the Baptist initiated "a religious movement that lasted beyond his death.[121] He further rightly emphasizes: "Most momentous was the influence that John exercised upon Jesus and his disciples."[122]

While the various items above in John's message seem clear, it is necessary to look at each of them in more detail because Jewish thought on most of these matters at the time of John the Baptist was ambiguous and not uniform. In addition, because of the geographical proximity of John the Baptist to the Qumran community and because of similarities of some concepts and ideas between them, it will be necessary to discuss Qumran and some of its ideas from time to time.[123] It may be useful then, at this point to summarize the history of the Qumran community. The following stages are fairly well established:[124]

700-600 B.C.E. Israelite Occupation

150-100 B.C.E. (Ia) Founding of the Essene Community

100-31 B.C.E. (Ib) Expansion of the Essene Community

31-4 B.C.E. Largely Abandoned

4 B.C.E. - 68 C.E.(II) Reoccupation by Essenes

69-74 C.E. (III) Roman Occupation

74-132 C.E. Unoccupied

132-135 C.E. Bar Cozebah Occupation

This sequence is established fundamentally by the archeological evidence of coins and remains of buildings on the site.[125] It is also generally agreed that the community in its various stages was Essene,[126] though after 6 C.E. there appears to be Zealot influence there as well.[127] The main cemetery contains some 1100 tombs nearly all male (with a few women and children in an extension area).[128]   Two other cemeteries, of 15 and 30 tombs each, "contained male, female and infant bodies. Very few of the individuals buried in these three cemeteries had passed their fortieth year."[129]

The main formative period of the community was Ib. Murphy-O'Connor writes: "An influx of new occupants made a building program imperative, and it is in this phase [100-31 B.C.E.] that Qumran acquired what was to be virtually its definitive form."[130] The virtual abandonment of the site ca. 31 B.C.E. has been variously explained. There is evidence of destruction of some of the buildings by earthquake and a subsequent fire.[131]   This destruction was not so extensive, however, as to require abandonment. A possible explanation may be that since Herod the Great favored the Essenes and appointed High Priests of Aaronic lineage,[132] the Qumran Essenes may have felt comfortable in returning to Jerusalem during his reign, instead of rebuilding. It may be significant that it was at the beginning of Herod's reign (39-34 B.C.E.) the Essene gate was built in the wall near the Temple precincts and an Essene settlement established in that area.[133]

The second major period of occupation of the Qumran site begins in 4 B.C.E. (II). All the evidence indicates it was reoccupied by the same group that had abandoned it earlier.[134] While there may have been some later influence from Zealots, at the time of this resettlement (ca 4 B.C.E.) they had not yet come into existence, having first arisen in connection with the 6 C.E. revolt against Archelaus.[135] Since Archelaus was antagonistic to the Essenes, it is not surprising that the community would leave Jerusalem once more for Qumran when Archelaus became Ethnarch of Judea and Samaria at the death of his father Herod the Great.

It is probably just before the reoccupation of Qumran that John the Baptist was born and it was during the very years that he was growing up in Judea (Luke 1:5, 8, 39) until his public ministry in 26/27 C.E. that the Qumran community was reoccupied and flourishing once more.[136] With this background, then, it may not be surprising to see in the following discussion how frequently John the Baptist has contacts with ideas found in the documents from Qumran.

The individual aspects of John's message that will be considered are: The nearness of the end time and John's eschatological outlook; nature and significance of his baptism and his call to repentance; the Coming One; the future baptism with the Holy Spirit and fire. First of all, John appears to hold the eschatological outlook which is dominant in the Old Testament and in Judaism before ca 300 B.C.E. It was generally quite simple: At some point in history God would intervene (the Day of the Lord, cf. e.g. Amos 5:18-20) and punish all evil doers. This is spoken of in two ways: God would do this without any human agent (e.g. Is. 2:2-4/Micah 4:1-4) or through a human leader, most often spoken of as of the line of David (e.g. Is. 9:2-7; 11:1-10).[137] This would end the present evil Age and bring in the endless New Age on a transformed earth. Only those faithful ones who happened to be alive at that time would share in this New Age.[138] This view is illustrated in the diagram below.

Neither in John's preaching, nor in the Qumran documents is there any evidence of an expectation that the dead would be raised either to be punished or to share in the New Age.[139]

Against this background John then sees himself as called by God a) to announce the imminent arrival of that great judgment and b) to prepare Israel for its arrival. It is striking that Mark 1:2, 3; Q (Lk 7:27/Matt. 11:10); John 1:23 all associate John's activity with Is. 40:3 and that this passage is the very one the Qumran community pointed to as an explanation of why they had gathered together in the wilderness area of the Dead Sea.[140] Given these contacts of John the Baptist with the eschatological expectations of the Qumran Essenes, in what way does he differ from them? One clear way is that *for them* the end time was still in the uncertain future; for John it was about to break forth. Fitzmyer posits that John the Baptist's call from God (Lk 3:2) "could be understood as a turning point when he broke off from the Essenes with whom he had lived for some time, and went forth to preach a baptism for the forgiveness of sins"[141] in preparation for the imminent day of judgment.

A different question is how did John the Baptist think of his role as one who prepares for the Lord's coming? The traditions are divided on this matter.   Did he think of himself as the Messiah—priestly or military? Or did he consider himself to be Elijah? There are three, or four if one includes Melchizedek,[142] eschatological figures thought to be expected by Qumran,[143] as well as by other Jews in the 1st century C.E. It is clear that Mark and Q and most subsequent Christian tradition identified John the Baptist with Elijah, who was to return and prepare the way for the Lord's coming.   Mark (1:2) does this by announcing John's appearance with a quotation of Mal. 3:1. Q has Jesus himself apply Mal. 3:1 to John (Lk. 7:24-28/Matt. 11:7-11). John's Gospel, however, has John the Baptist explicitly deny that he is Elijah *redivivus* (1:21). Whether or not John the Baptist ever thought of himself as a Messiah (perhaps the priestly one of Qumran, since he is of priestly lineage according to traditions in Luke), a continuing Baptist sect claimed him to be so.[144] There can be little doubt that those who came out to see this strange figure in the desert of Judea could not help but wonder how he fit into the scheme of various figures connected with the coming New Age which he proclaimed that God was about to bring in.

John's Baptism

The baptizing activity of John was so characteristic of him that it is witnessed to in all strands of the tradition and became the title by which he is distinguished from the many others in Palestine who bore this most common of Jewish names. The origin of this practice and its exact significance, however, is not without uncertainty.

While earlier it was customary to explain the origin of John's baptism (as well as later Christian baptism) by reference to proselyte baptism,[145] 1st Christian century evidence for proselyte baptism is uncertain.[146] It seems more correct to locate John's practice, as Fitzmyer does, "in the general baptist movement known to have existed in Palestine roughly between 150 B.C.E. and 250 C.E."[147] Jeremias notes: "Conjectures of a most varied kind have been made about the nature of John's baptism, but a satisfactory religious setting has yet to be found."[148] He then continues: "It is most probable that we should think of Essene influences. The very nearness of the place of baptism to Qumran makes the assumption of relationships between the two a likely one."[149] An unresolved aspect is that John's baptism was a one-time experience, whereas Qumran's washings were frequent. This may be due, however, to John's conviction that the New Age is about to dawn. Jeremias notes the Jewish eschatological expectation of an immersion at the end time similar to their earlier Exodus experience, as witnessed to, in his opinion, also by Paul in 1 Cor. 10:1f.[150] as a possible explanation for a *one-time* baptism.

Whatever the origin of John's baptism the traditions indicate that people were to undergo it as a sign that they accepted John as an authentic spokesman for God and that in truth he announced God's imminent bringing in of the New Age and its attendant eschatological judgment. A further significance to the acceptance of his baptism was that they were thereby preparing themselves to share in the blessings of the New Age by this cleansing bath and by its incumbent requirement of a changed life.[151]

The Coming One Who Baptizes with the Holy Spirit and with Fire

The term "Coming One" is ambiguous. In the Old Testament and in Judaism just before the time of John the Baptist the term can be used in a variety of ways.[152] It has been suggested that originally the phrase referred to God as the One who comes in eschatological judgment.[153] This does not seem probable as John's viewpoint in the light of John's later question in Q to Jesus: "Are you the One who is to come, or do we look for someone else?" (Luke 7:19; Matt. 11:3); as well as the strongly attested, very Semitic phrase John the Baptist uses describing the Coming One: "of whom I am not able to loose the *strap of his sandal.*"[154]

More frequently it is proposed that John the Baptist thought of Elijah *redivivus* as the future one who comes in fiery judgment.[155] This would mean, then, that John did not think of himself as Elijah and would agree with the Johannine view (John 1:21), but it would disagree with the Matthean and Markan view where John the Baptist is explicitly identified with Elijah (cf. Matthew's form of Q in 11:15 and Mark 9:11-13). This became the common Christian interpretation of John's role. The most common interpretation of the Coming One is that John meant it to refer to the expected Messiah—usually understood to be the Davidic Messiah.[156]

It is not possible to be certain what John's expectation specifically was beyond the fact that it is more probable that a human figure, rather than God, was his expectation; and that it would have been the Messiah, rather than Elijah, whom John envisioned as the agent of God's eschatological judgment and destruction of all evil doers. In any case, whatever John the Baptist anticipated, those who came to him would have had much cause to speculate as to who exactly would come and bring in the judgment and the New Age. Jesus also would have shared this uncertainty as he came and listened to John at the Jordan.

The Coming One John proclaims will baptize with the Holy Spirit (Mark 1:8) or with the Holy Spirit and fire (Q Luke 3:16; Matt. 3:11). Since Jesus' later actions do not fit the judgmental implications of the Q account, it is most likely that the Q account reflects John's actual preaching which Mark has modified somewhat to correspond to what he presents Jesus as doing.[157]   The term baptism here is clearly metaphorical and refers, in the case of the Holy Spirit, to the fact that the Coming One inaugurates the New Age, which is the Age of the Spirit (cf. Joel 3:1ff.).[158] In addition to the prophetic aspect clear from Joel 3 it may also refer to the cleansing, sanctifying aspect of the Spirit's activity in the New Age (Ezek. 36 e.g.). This cleansing can be viewed both individually and also as a refining and purifying of the nation of Israel by the destruction of evildoers in its midst.[159]

The judgment aspect comes out even more clearly in the Q form which speaks of a baptism of fire and then continues with the metaphor of the Coming One winnowing grain and burning up the chaff with unquenchable fire (Lk. 3:17; Matt. 3:12). This combination of the Holy Spirit, baptism, and judgment which characterizes John the Baptist's message has close parallels with the Qumran literature[160] and, as Fitzmyer notes: "This makes it plausible that John did spend some time in his youth with the Essenes and that his ideas... were influenced by this experience."[161]

It may be noted that the ethical advice John gives in Luke 3:10-14 may be either from Q (preserved only by Luke) or from Luke's special material.[162]

Jesus' Baptism by John

One of the most certain events in the life of the historical Jesus is that he was baptized by John the Baptist.[163] This was found by the early Church to be very offensive;[164] and its unease is reflected in the Gospels in various ways.[165] Thus there can be little doubt that Jesus, like many pious Jews of his day, was drawn to John's preaching and baptizing sometime in the period ca 26-28 C.E.[166] It is said in Luke's Gospel that he was about 30 years of age (Lk 3:23), which may reflect an early tradition.[167]

Why would Jesus leave Galilee and come to John who is preaching and baptizing in Judea at the Jordan (Mark 1:9)? There are a number of possibilities. John's preaching was attracting crowds[168] and Jesus no doubt heard of him and his message. If, as Luke's traditions suggest, he and John were near relatives, this would be an added incentive for Jesus to go to hear him. Whatever the reason, there is no indication in any of the earliest traditions that Jesus thought of himself at this time of having any special role[169] in relation to God's plans for the New Age. Rather, merely as one pious Jew among many such Jesus comes to learn whether John is indeed a prophet sent from God and speaks God's message. The fact that Jesus chooses to undergo John's baptism is a clear indication that he accepts the validity of John's role and message.[170] There are other indications that Jesus recognized John's authenticity as God's spokesman at this crisis time in world history. First of all, there is Jesus' statement in Q (Lk. 7:28; Matt. 11:11) and the Gospel of Thomas (46) about the surpassing greatness of John.[171] Further, the rabbinic-like dispute,[172] which Jesus has with the religious authorities in Jerusalem (Mark 11:27-33) and in which they question Jesus' authority, clearly shows Jesus' view that John's baptism and ministry were authentically God's will and that the religious leaders, like Jesus and the pious ordinary people, should have undergone it, indicating thereby their own acceptance of John and his ministry.

All of this means that Jesus also accepted John's proclamation of the imminent inbreaking of the Kingdom of God. Schweizer correctly notes that by going to John for baptism: "This in itself makes it extremely likely that Jesus too, took as his point of departure expectation of the coming kingdom of God."[173]   Sanders agrees and emphasizes the centrality of eschatology for understanding Jesus own ministry.[174] It is this eschatological outlook that provides the context for Jesus' initial meeting with John, and it is the eschatological context which colors the developments to be noted in Jesus' subsequent thinking.

Jesus' Awareness of His Special Role

In connection with Jesus' being baptized, unexpectedly a momentous event occurs according to the traditions—Jesus comes to an awareness that God has a special role for him in the New Age whose nearness John is announcing. This is indicated in a variety of ways in the Gospels. While the Synoptic accounts (Matthew and Luke clearly dependent on the Markan story) do not show John the Baptist pointing to Jesus as the expected One at the time of his baptism, John's Gospel plainly states that the Baptist did recognize and point to Jesus as the one who comes after him and baptizes with the Holy Spirit (1:30-34). Even though the language and concepts of the Johannine account may be more those of the Gospel writer than of the Baptist, there are a number of factors that make it probable that John the Baptist did at some point recognize Jesus as the One he expected to come.[175] First of all, it has been suggested that here, as elsewhere in the Fourth Gospel, there are earlier traditions not used by the Synoptics.[176] Further, the question of John through his disciples in Q "Are you the Coming One?" suggests that John had earlier considered Jesus to be that person. The fact that the Synoptics do not explicitly note in connection with Jesus' baptism any statement of John the Baptist concerning Jesus' role in the coming Kingdom is probably to be understood as another indication of the hesitancy on the part of the Gospel writers to give John too important a role in Jesus' own development and awareness of his mission.[177] Thus while there cannot be absolute certainty that John the Baptist at the time of Jesus' baptism declared him to be the Coming One,[178] all the Gospel accounts agree that in some way Jesus became aware that he had some special role at this time. This awareness is reflected in the Gospels' mention of a heavenly voice and the descent of the Holy Spirit.[179] In John's account these 2 items are given as evidence to John the Baptist who then publicly declares Jesus' special role (1:33f.); in Mark (1:10f.) the voice is addressed to Jesus using the words of Ps. 2:7 and the Spirit is said to descend "as a dove;" in Matthew (3:16f.) the voice speaks in the third person about Jesus; Luke (3:22) has the saying in the second person like Mark, but adds that the descent of the Spirit was "in *bodily form* as a dove." In all three Synoptic accounts it is Jesus who is said to have seen the Spirit's descent; whereas in John it is the Baptist who sees it (1:32).

How is this divergency to be understood? They seem to be different ways of speaking (in very early strands of tradition) about either an inner experience of Jesus at the moment of his baptism, or of a vision he had at that time. That Jesus seems to have had such visionary experiences is suggested by a number of other incidents mentioned in the Gospels. In Luke 10:18 Jesus says "I saw Satan as a star falling out of heaven." This is either a part of Luke's special tradition or a part of the Q block that follows (Lk.10:21-24; Matt. 11:25-27; 13:16,17) which Matthew has omitted. It is very Semitic Greek.[180] In an independent Johannine tradition Jesus describes a voice he heard from heaven (12:28-30).[181] Finally, while the nature of the transfiguration experience of Jesus (Mk. 9:2-8; Lk. 9:28-30; Matt. 17:1-8) is uncertain,[182] one possible explanation is that originally it was a visionary experience of Jesus which in the process of transmission of the traditions becomes witnessed to by the disciples as well. In any case it is striking, as Jeremias notes, that in the 5 independent lines of tradition[183] concerning Jesus' baptism "all the texts agree in reporting two things: the descent of the spirit and a proclamation associated with it."[184] The quotation of the Psalms passage as well as the specific titles assigned in the Gospel accounts to Jesus in that connection (Son, Servant, Lamb of God) are best understood as evidence of later Christian interpretations of the tradition.[185] Jesus' subsequent action immediately[186] following his baptism (Mark 1:12 and pars; Q) of going off by himself into the deserted area around the Jordan, indicates the profound effect this experience had upon him; and in the light of the great diversity of Jewish expectations concerning the New Age it is not surprising that his experiences there in the wilderness reflect a tremendous struggle, variously interpreted in the traditions as his temptation/testing. This struggle will be studied in the subsequent chapters but already at this juncture Jesus had to integrate into his thinking and world view a) that the long-awaited New Age was dawning and b) his own role over against it and over against John the Baptist's ministry.

Chapter 3

From Baptism to the Imprisonment
of John

In various ways each of the Gospels takes notice of the fact that John the Baptist has been put in prison, indicating thereby that this event was in some way essentially connected to Jesus' own life and activity, and that it was so firmly imbedded in the tradition that it could not be disregarded.

The way it is referred to in Luke's and John's Gospels reveals that the Baptist's imprisonment was felt by them to be a problem. Luke mentions it just *before* the baptism of Jesus (3:19ff.), using this strange placement to make less obvious that it was John who actually baptized Jesus—avoiding in this way any apparent dependence on or subordination of Jesus himself to John, but also softening the impression Mark gives (1:14) that somehow Jesus' ministry is dependent on and continues the earlier ministry of John the Baptist.[187]

The Fourth Gospel knows of the tradition of the imprisonment of the Baptist and cannot disregard it either; but by only noting it in an off-hand manner (3:24) the writer prevents any activity of John (subsequent to John's declaring Jesus to be Messiah) from appearing to be influential in Jesus' decisions.

The Synoptics recount only one event in this period—the "temptation" of Jesus. John's Gospel, on the other hand, makes no mention of this at all, but instead devotes a considerable amount of space to Jesus' activity back and forth throughout Palestine, carrying out a ministry that at times seems to parallel and also conflict with that of John the Baptist (cf. 3:22ff.; 4:1ff.).

From all the Gospels, then, it is clear there was an indeterminate period of time between the baptism of Jesus and the imprisonment of the Baptist who had initiated in Israel the expectation of the near end of the present Age and the dawn of the Messianic era. Further, where Jesus was during this time and what he was doing is variously represented—little or no information about his activity and the implication that he spent all this time in Judea in the Synoptics; considerable activity both in Galilee and Judea in John. Finally, while all note the imprisonment of John, none of the Gospels gives any indication of *why* that event was important either in general or for Jesus himself.[188]

As will be seen some insight into Jesus' understanding during this period of the part he is to play in God's plan for the New Age can be gained both by a study of the "temptation" accounts in the Synoptics and the traditions of Jesus' activity in John's Gospel. The use of Johannine material, however, needs further consideration at this point. While all scholars recognize that the theology of the writer of the Fourth Gospel has thoroughly colored the presentation and language of the Gospel—particularly evident in the discourses,[189] nevertheless the narratives in the Gospel are seldom free creations of the writer but rather his use of traditions which are independent of the Synoptics.[190]

In general the practice to be followed below will be that where John and the Synoptics agree there is to be seen evidence of earlier traditions being used by both independently. In the case of unique Johannine events narrated with a high degree of Semitic coloring and where the text is dissimilar from what might be expected in the early Palestinian church, this will also suggest that the material may go back to the time of Jesus and his disciples. Chronological sequence of events will need to be decided on a case to case basis, with no preference being accorded *a priori* either to John or to the Synoptics.[191]

Concerning the duration of Jesus' public activity after his baptism, while it is generally clear that the Synoptic picture of one year is too compressed and the Johannine scheme of three (or four) passovers is possibly a literary structure, a ministry of 2 or 3 years is most probable.[192] Further, attested by both John and the Synoptics, there was a stay in *Judea* after his baptism of an indeterminate length and about which John's Gospel has apparently some independent traditions.

Jesus' Struggle in the Wilderness

This story has been designated either as the "temptation" or the "testing" of Jesus. In the traditions it is presented as Jesus' being impelled by God's Spirit (Mk. 1:13; Matt. 4:1; Lk. 4:1) into the wilderness area of Judea (cf. Lk. 4:1) and struggling there with Satan, the leader of the demonic powers opposing God's plans and will. While both "testing" and "temptation" correctly translate the Greek *peirazo,* if the moving power behind Jesus' struggle here is viewed primarily as God, then "testing" is more appropriate. If the activity of Satan is more in view, "temptation" would be better. Jeremias, however, is correct in suggesting that rather than either, the story should be viewed primarily as the "ordeal" or struggle of Jesus.[193]

The tradition is doubly attested (Mk. 1:12f. and Q: Mt. 4:1-11; Lk. 4:1-13) and placed by Crossan in his first stratum (30-60 C.E.).[194] The Markan account is the earliest form of the tradition[195]—merely stating the fact of an extended period spent alone in the wilderness, viewed as a Spirit motivated struggle with Satan. As Jeremias points out: "Consideration of the individual details confirms that the Matthean/Lucan version reflects a later stage of the tradition."[196] While Crossan places the Q material as a whole in first *stratum* (30-60 C.E.), he considers the Q temptation story to belong to the third and latest *layer* of the Q source.[197]

It is necessary at this point to say a bit more about the Q source. Any attempt to understand that source must take into account both its Greek and its Semitic features. While it is generally agreed that there was a Semitic stage in the transmission of Q traditions, there is no agreement as to whether this stage was only oral or also produced written Semitic (Aramaic) forms of any of the traditions. After an extended survey Kloppenborg concludes "that while parts of Q betray a Semitizing Greek style, and possibly an origin in an Aramaic-speaking milieu, there is no convincing proof of a literary formulation in Aramaic."[198] While he correctly notes that the Greek verbal agreements between Matthew and Luke in their Q material "compel us to assume that the two evangelists at least had before them a Greek copy of Q,"[199] he undervalues the significance and extent of the syntactical features which betray the Semitic substratum of the Q material.[200] In his analysis of a number of syntactical features[201] Kloppenborg considers only the statistics for Q material *as a whole,* whereas a careful study shows that *Semitic syntactical features occur predominantly in some of the sayings and narratives of Q and not in others* and thus each smaller unit needs consideration by itself. This is not surprising for it is clear that Q contains a variety of earlier traditions each of which had its own transmission history before being taken up into the Q collection. Another aspect needs consideration also—while Matthew and Luke often agree in the over all Semitic nature of the Q material, at times one will be highly Semitized and the other less so or not at all. These phenomena do not become apparent when statistics for Q as a whole are only considered and thus Kloppenborg's conclusion does not adequately represent the situation. He writes: "Were there earlier recensions in Aramaic? The evidence for this is not strong... syntactical analysis provides good evidence of non-translation Greek. In this light the most economical solution is this: Q was compiled and composed in Greek."[202] As will be seen from Appendix 1 ("Syntax Criticism of Q"), 21 of the 36 units in Q show up as translation Greek in either Matthew or Luke or both, that is 58% of the Q material.[203] This *highly Semitized Greek* is found in all three layers of Q—the Sapiential (61%), the Apocalyptic (53%), and in the temptation account as preserved in Luke.[204] While there is no doubt that Matthew and Luke had Q in front of them in Greek as Kloppenborg insists, it is also clear that in their use of that document, Matthew and Luke have often preserved evidence of earlier Semitic stages of those traditions: Luke does so 53% of the time; Matthew 28%.   They agree in having translation Greek frequencies in 22% of their common tradition.

Luke's form of the "temptation" story (4:1-13) is one of the most Semitic of the Q traditions;[205] and while it may have been attached to the Q source in the later stages,[206] the temptation account of Luke clearly was not originally composed in Greek and in its Greek dress still reveals its earlier Semitic, Palestinian roots.[207]

While it is generally conceded, then, that behind both the Q and the Markan accounts some actual experience of solitary struggle of Jesus is evident, the nature of this experience is variously understood. Jeremias[208] and others[209] consider that Jesus felt himself to be in a very real and concrete struggle vs Satan and his evil forces. The issue, however, is whether or not the stories reflect such an actuality *at the time of Jesus' baptism* or whether the accounts have compressed into this point Jesus' subsequent view (or the view of the early Church), as experienced throughout the years of his later ministry. Jeremias seems to hold that already at this initial time Jesus felt both that he had engaged Satan and "vanquished" him. He writes: "Thus it is highly probable that here, too [Lk. 11:21f.] we have a piece of pre-Easter tradition. In this parable of the duel, the binding of the strong man evidently *alludes to a particular event: Jesus can only mean the overcoming of the temptation depicted in Mark 1:12f.* [italics added]."[210]

It is, however, more probable that while at this early stage in Jesus' ministry he anticipated a very real struggle between God and God's people and Satan and his forces in this New Age which John declared was dawning, the *sense of victory* over Satan which the temptation account in Q announces more probably reflects Jesus' later experiences as he finds himself engaged in this struggle throughout his ministry, as Fitzmyer suggests.[211] It may be significant that the less developed form of the tradition in Mark (1:12f.) only speaks of *struggle* vs Satan, not of any victory.[212]

As indicated above Jesus, like most of his contemporaries,[213] expected to be engaged in a real struggle in the New Age against demonic forces opposed to God and spoke about that struggle as he carried out his later ministry. It is more probable, however, at this *earliest point* in his awareness of the near-arrival of God's reign, that the struggle at this time for Jesus would be more along the lines of "Is John correct that it is near? Is John correct that I am to play a special role in its arriving? If so, what is that role?" The answers he would give to those questions Jesus knew would involve him in a very real struggle with Satanic powers,[214] and so these were momentous issues for him. From this moment onwards Jesus had to view all that happens to him and in the world from an *eschatological* viewpoint—God's New Age was becoming a reality and this required commitment by all to this super-human struggle. What that involves for him he not surprisingly would feel needed to be explored in a period of isolation and prayer; and it is this which these "temptation/testing/struggle" traditions indicate.

What will this New Age be like? What role am I to carry out? How am I to do this? These were questions for which a Jewish person at that time had no generally agreed upon answers. Particularly the human leadership God would use to carry out his plans was variously understood, as well as the means which they were to employ.[215] Would it be a priest; a Davidic military and political leader? Would it involve open revolt against Rome or would it come about by more direct action of God himself? This question concerning the nature of the Messianic leadership seems to have split the Pharisee party sometime after 50 B.C.E.[216] and surely by 6 C.E., the first recorded appearance of the Zealots.[217] It appears that at that time the more politically inclined Pharisees joined the radical Judas the Galilean in an abortive attempt to throw off the Roman yoke and thus there were those who saw violence as God's way of establishing the New Age.[218] Even more violent were the Sicarii, characterized by Horsley as "an urban group engaged in terrorist activities, such as assassination... of high priests who were collaborating with Roman rule..."[219]

The language of the "temptation" in Q has led to the view that at this early stage Jesus both wrestled with the question of whether political Messiahship was to be his role and that he also rejected it.[220] It is questionable if this is so. The first 2 temptations in Matthew's account (concerning food and casting himself down from the top of the Temple) suggest a temptation to seek divine powers for personal security and self glorification. At this point, however, there is no indication that Jesus was aware of having any special access to divine power and thus this wording seems to reflect expectations that Jesus might have had later in his public ministry when miraculous manifestations do occur. The 3rd temptation (to worship Satan and so rule) does have, however, political overtones. Given the widespread Jewish expectations at this time, Jesus would surely at some point, no doubt, have had to consider whether his was to be such a political role.[221] There was nothing, however, in John's preaching (as far as can be gleaned from the accounts) to cause Jesus to think along such political lines. It is more probable that John, of priestly lineage with some evident Essene-Qumran leanings, would have been concerned with the wickedness of the Temple hierarchy and its practices rather than with political action or revolt.[222]

Whatever conclusions Jesus may have reached in this period of isolation immediately after his baptism one thing is clear—both the Synoptics and John's Gospel show him as not immediately undertaking a mission independent of John. This is surprising. Jesus' period of inactivity and silence in Judea as implied by the Synoptics is surely unexpected, as is also the Johannine view that Jesus after his baptism was for a time a *follower* of John the Baptist. The *Synoptic* picture makes little sense if Jesus in the wilderness reached certainty of conviction about the arrival of the Kingdom and his role in it. The

Johannine picture is surprising since it leaves the impression of Jesus' subordination to John, which could only be problematic for the early Church. Both traditions, however, are understandable if at this stage Jesus is still uncertain about God's plan and continues to follow the one whom God is using to announce his plans, waiting expectantly for the Kingdom to arrive.

The Fourth Gospel, in contrast to the Synoptics, avoids making John's imprisonment determinative for Jesus' own actions, but cannot disregard a fact so strongly imbedded in the tradition. Thus, as an aside, the writer notes in 3:24 that John the Baptist has not yet been arrested,[223] showing he had traditions before this event of Jesus continuing to follow John (1:29ff.) also after his baptism (1:35ff.; 3:25);[224] attracting followers to himself from the group around John (1:37);[225] and travelling back and forth between Judea and Galilee (1:43; 2:13; 3:22).[226]

Three items from the Johannine picture of Jesus in this period, however, require further comment: a) Did Jesus engage in baptizing activity while in Judea before John's imprisonment? b) Did Jesus perform any miracles during this period? c) Did Jesus "cleanse" the Temple during this period?

Did Jesus Baptize before the Imprisonment of John?

The only references to Jesus baptizing are the brief notices in John 3:22-26 and 4:1, though the second of these is quickly followed by the disclaimer (4:2) "Jesus himself did not baptize, but only his disciples." The disclaimer itself, however, probably indicates the existence of an early tradition that Jesus did indeed baptize. Brown has stated the case well: "There is no plausible theological reason why anyone would have invented the tradition that Jesus and his disciples once baptized... as a matter of fact, the information that Jesus once imitated John the Baptist in baptizing would be a dangerous weapon in the hands of the sectarians of John the Baptist (whence probably the modification in iv. 2)."[227]

Did Jesus Perform Any Miracles during This Early Period?

The only miracle specifically recounted in this period by the Fourth Gospel is that of the changing of water into wine (2:1-12). This is said to have occurred in Cana of Galilee and if it reflects traditional material[228] need not necessarily have occurred in the period *prior* to John's imprisonment. The only other possible indications of any miraculous activity on Jesus' part before the imprisonment of John are the references to "signs" which Jesus is said to have performed in Jerusalem in John 2:23 and 3:2. The word 'sign', however, is a technical term of the writer of the Fourth Gospel for miracles of Jesus which reveal his glory[229] and most probably reflects his theological/literary interest here and does not contain any tradition-recollection of miraculous activity in Jerusalem at this early stage.[230]

Did Jesus Cleanse the Temple during This Period?

The location of the account of the cleansing of the Temple differs in the Synoptic Gospels and in John. In the former it is narrated in connection with the Triumphal Entry just before the last Passover during which Jesus was crucified, whereas in John it is narrated at the beginning of the Gospel, in connection with another Passover some three years earlier. Most commentators accept the Synoptic placing as correct and consider John's arrangement to be the result of theological and literary considerations.[231] It may well be argued, however, that the location in John's Gospel has at least as much inherent probability of being correct as that of the Synoptics.[232]

The Markan chronology is obviously compressed and in a number of places Mark's material is grouped topically rather than being in chronological order, e.g. the conflict stories (2:1-3:5), the parable section (4:1-34) and the 'Little Apocalypse' (Chapter 13).[233] The Johannine placement, on balance, is more probable than the Markan, as Fitzmyer concludes, noting that

> the one incident in the gospel tradition which associated him with violence is precisely this episode, and it would more plausibly have been associated with the beginning of the ministry. For this reason I should prefer to think of the basic episode as having a context early in Jesus' ministry in Stage I of the gospel tradition... the Synoptics would have related it to the end of ministry, because in their tradition that is the only time Jesus arrives in Jerusalem and comes in contact with the Temple.[234]

Another feature which favors the Johannine location rather than the Markan is the remarkable correlation of the dating notice in v. 20 of the Johannine account (26-28 C.E.) and the probable date of Jesus' early activity in Judea.[235] The relationship of John 2:18-22 to the Temple incident (2:13-17) is not agreed upon. As the material is presented in John's Gospel there are clearly three units: (1) The Narrative of the Cleansing (vv. 13-17); (2) The Dispute (vv. 18-20); (3) The Writer's Explanatory Comment (vv. 21,22). Bultmann maintains that vv. 13-19 belong together and represent with some modifications a Semitic written source taken over by the Evangelist.[236] He notes as Semitic the way vv. 14, 18 and 19 begin, as well as certain details in the narration, such as the fact that the sellers are seated (v. 14) and that a whip is used (v. 15).[237] Dodd also argues for the original unity of the narration of the cleansing (vv. 13-17) and the logion (vv. 18, 19) which the author of the Fourth Gospel preserves, but which Mark did not.[238] That vv. 21,22 are the Gospel writer's explanatory comment is clear. It is not clear, however, why v. 20 should be separated from vv. 13-19 and taken with v. 21 as Bultmann does.[239] In style and form v. 20 is more parallel to v. 18 than it is either to v. 17 or v. 21 which Bultmann correctly understands as comments of the writer.[240] Further in vv. 19 and 20 'temple' refers to the actual Jerusalem Temple, whereas in v. 21 (the writer's comment) 'temple' is given a second meaning, the body of Jesus, in line with the common Johannine technique of double meanings observable in chapters 3, 4, 6.

It would seem that the most probable understanding of John 2:13-22 is that vv. 13-16, 18-20 came to the writer as a unit of early tradition and that vv. 17 and 21f. are his comments upon it. The date indicated by v. 20 is then at the same time the date of the Temple cleansing, with which it was connected in the tradition used by the author of the Gospel: that is, the cleansing of the Temple in John 2 took place in 26-28 C.E. If a choice then must be made between the Synoptic and the Johannine location, the scales are tipped in favor of the Johannine; and its connection in the Synoptics with the final week of Jesus' life is to be understood as the result of Mark's regrouping of the material.

It is generally agreed that the Johannine account here is independent of the Synoptics[241] and, as Bultmann has noted, it goes back to a Semitic tradition.[242] Crossan places this multiply attested tradition into his earliest stage and concludes "that an action and equal saying involving the Temple's symbolic destruction goes back to the historical Jesus himself..."[243]

How is this action to be understood in the light of Jesus' thinking at this early stage in his awareness of his call to join with John the Baptist in waiting for and announcing the nearness of the Kingdom's arrival?[244]

It is not probable, as Anderson correctly notes, that Jesus here intended to engage in any political or revolutionary act; nor do the traditions indicate he was leading a group of like-minded followers.[245]   Rather, Anderson suggests: "Far from a major military or political or reform exploit having been 'denatured' in the story, it appears much more likely that what was originally a minor episode in a corner of the Temple court has been magnified in the tradition and developed according to the theological predilections of the Evangelists."[246]

What then may have been Jesus' intention? It is best understood as a symbolic act[247] indicating that the Temple and its leadership, as well as the nation in general needed to be made ready for the New Age. Did this involve a reform of the Temple or its *destruction*?[248]   Jewish expectations concerning the fate of the Temple in the Messianic age were varied. Sanders has summarized the situation well:

> This rapid survey of passages does not lead to the conclusion that all Jews everywhere, when thinking of the future hope of Israel, put foremost the building of a new Temple. Further, when the Temple is explicitly mentioned, it is not depicted in a uniform manner. To be more precise, sometimes it is not depicted at all (2 Macc. 2:7; Jub. 1:17, 27; 11 Q Temple 29:8-10), and sometimes it appears that the present second Temple is in mind (1 En. 25:5; II Macc. 2:7). Sometimes the new Temple is modestly expected only to be larger and grander than the present Temple (Tob. 14:5 'glorious'; 1 En. 90:28f. 'greater and loftier'; T. Benj. 9:2 'more glorious than the first')... In some instances it is definitely said or clearly implied that God will build or provide a new Temple (1 En. 90:28f.; Jub. 1:17; 11 Q Temple 29:8-18) and in Sib. Or. 5:425 the builder 'is a blessed man from heaven.' Thus we can speak of neither a universal expectation nor a clear and consistent one.[249]

It may well be, then, that all Jesus, in keeping with the prophet Malachi, intended to show was the need for a deep renewal and cleansing of the Temple and its practices.[250]

In this connection it may be pointed out that the cleansing of the Temple occurring in close proximity to the Passover (whether it be the first, as in John, or the last as in the Synoptics) falls very near to, if not on, the first of the two days appointed in Ezekiel for the *ritual cleansing* of the Temple. According to Ezekiel 45:18 a ritual cleansing of the Temple was to be made on the first day of the first month (Nisan 1) in preparation for the Passover on Nisan 14; and according   to

Ezekiel 45:20 a ritual cleansing of the temple was again to be made on the first day of the seventh month (Tishri 1).[251]

The Gospel of John only remarks that the Passover 'was near', but it may very well be that Jesus chose the very day some two weeks before Passover on which the Temple was being *ritually* cleansed as the occasion for his dramatic action. In fact the suggestion to carry out his own cleansing of the Temple may have come to Jesus as the result of the lessons which he had no doubt heard read in the Synagogue on the previous Sabbath. This Sabbath was called *Hahodesh* and the lessons appointed to be read each year on this day in the earliest lectionary system of the Synagogue were Exodus 12:2-20, the *Seder* reading, and as the *Haphtarah* reading Ezekiel 45:18-46, which gives the regulation concerning the ritual cleansing of the Temple discussed above.[252] From his earliest days Jesus had heard this portion from Ezekiel read. What would be more natural than for him to be led by this Scripture to demonstrate graphically that something more than a merely ritual cleansing of the Temple was required!

Whether this action of Jesus and any subsequent reaction from the Temple authorities played a role in Jesus' eventually leaving Judea to announce the Kingdom's arrival in Galilee is not clear. Both the obduracy of the Jerusalem hierarchy[253] and John the Baptist's Judean ministry being cut short by his arrest may have been for Jesus an indication that God was calling[254] him to continue John's work in Galilee.[255] In any case it is in Galilee, according to the traditions, that Jesus' distinctive ministry and message take shape.

Chapter 4

From John's Imprisonment to John's Death

As noted in the previous chapter the arrest of John the Baptist is considered somehow significant for the witness to Jesus in all the Gospels[256] and, further, Jesus himself appears to have found in that event an indication that he is called by God to go to Galilee and proclaim the nearness[257] of the Kingdom (Mark 1:15). Although it appears that for a while Jesus proclaims a message similar to that of John the Baptist, eventually he comes to a different understanding of the New Age and its implications.[258] It is the changes which occur in this period between the arrest and the death of John which will be discussed in this chapter.

The difficulty in arriving at any consensus concerning Jesus' thinking/speaking about the Kingdom of God is due partly to the fact that the Gospel materials speak of the Kingdom in four ways: as future, as present, as hidden, as being associated with a cataclysmic world judgment.[259] Rather than choosing one of these over the others as being what the historical Jesus thought and spoke about,[260] the correct solution lies more in understanding that changes seem to have occurred in Jesus' own thinking about the Kingdom.[261]

The material in the Gospels is not arranged chronologically, nor with the intent to show such development in Jesus' thinking about the coming Kingdom and his own role. Yet a careful reading of the Gospel material does indicate some changes are taking place.[262] There appear to be two clearly defined stages in this early period of his Galilean ministry[263]—I. Jesus' initial proclamation (very similar to John's) that the Kingdom is very near; II. His subsequent conviction and proclamation that the Kingdom *has arrived.*

I. *Jesus' Early Proclamation of the Kingdom's Imminent Coming*

It may be that because of the imprisonment of God's messenger, John, Jesus felt the coming was more imminent than it had been.[264] While John the Baptist appears to have held the Old Testament view that the New Age would be ushered in by one mighty cataclysmic act of divine judgment,[265] other Jews looked forward to a two stage process with an initial eradication of evil followed by a temporary Messianic[266] rule on earth, which in turn would be followed by the final cataclysmic judgment ushering in a new heaven and a new earth—as, for example, in 1 Enoch 91-94:[267] The first 7 weeks (93:2-9) recount the world's history up to the war of judgment carried out in the 8th week "on the oppressors, and sinners shall be delivered into the hands of the righteous (91:12):[268] Then follows a period of materialistic Messianic bliss (91:13), which continues into the 9th week when "all the deeds of the sinners shall depart from upon the whole earth" (91:15). In the 7th part of the 10th week the great eternal judgment occurs, carried out by the angels and then "the first heaven shall depart and pass away" and "a new heaven shall appear" (91:16). "Then after that there shall be many weeks without number forever" (91:17).[269] It is clear that at some point in Jesus' ministry some who held hopes similar to those of Enoch joined themselves to Jesus; and thus Jesus himself, as followers gather around him, would have had to consider which world view was correct and whether it would include a temporary Messianic age on earth.[270] Related to that question would be to what extent would God himself bring in that rule and to what extent would God use human agents and violence to accomplish it?[271]

Jesus appears to have agreed with the Pharisees against the Zealots that violent political revolution initiated by human beings was not the way of God's establishing his rule, for a) there is no evidence of any advocacy of violence in the traditions preserved[272] and b) Jesus contrasts his own ministry with that of John's when he replies concerning John's question from prison: "From the days of John the Baptist until now the kingdom of heaven has suffered violence, and men of violence take it by force" (Matt. 11:12; Luke 16:16). Further he rejects the suggestion that he call down God's judgment on those who reject him and his message (Mk. 9:54f.). This is not surprising, for in this stage at least Jesus, like John, is certain it is God who will take the initiative in determining when and how the Kingdom is to arrive.

There is little indication of Jesus' thinking in other areas, but a distinctive ministry and message does become apparent eventually. There is no evidence that Jesus continued a baptizing ministry in Galilee, but the reasons for his not continuing this aspect are nowhere mentioned. If John's baptism, however, was largely thought of in terms of ritual washings such as were common at Qumran, Jesus' discontinuing that aspect may be an early evidence[273] of Jesus' freer attitude toward the ritual—more in line with that of the *'am-ha-aretz* than that of the Essenes or Pharisees. Sanders correctly notes that "The common people ['*am-ha-aretz*] were not irreligious. They presumably kept most of the law most of the time, observed the festivals, and paid heed to some of the more serious purity regulations. It was only the special purity laws of the *haberim* which they did not observe."[274] Jesus, like John, welcomed these people when they rejoiced at the news that the Kingdom was about to arrive (Matt. 21:31f.; Luke 3:12; 7:29). Jesus differs from John, also, in not living the life of an ascetic, as can be seen from the Q passage (Luke 7:33f.; Matt. 11:18f.) where Jesus declares that, in contrast to John, he is being called "a glutton and a drunkard."[275]

In this period Jesus would be attracting followers, some of whom seem to have made his acquaintance already in Judea as both he and they followed John the Baptist. Sometime also during this period when John the Baptist is in prison Jesus begins to experience the ability to perform miracles;[276] and it was particularly his ability to cast out demons which, according to the tradition (Q: Lk. 11:20/Matt. 12:28; Mk. 3:23-27), indicated to Jesus that the Kingdom he and John had been proclaiming had arrived.[277] This realization radically changes Jesus' expectations and message.

II. *Jesus' Conviction and Proclamation that the Kingdom Has Arrived.*

In a number of passages in the Synoptics Jesus clearly states that the Kingdom has arrived.[278] One of the most important is the response of Jesus in Q to the charge that he casts out demons by Beelzebul (Lk. 11:20; Matt. 12:28). There Jesus says "But if I by the finger (Matt. "Spirit") of God cast out demons, then the Kingdom of God *has come upon you.*" The Greek verb here is *phthanō* which means "just arrived, arrive, come."[279] Crossan lists this passage in his "first stratum" of material and marks it with +, indicating his view that it is "from the historical Jesus."[280]   Since this conception of the Kingdom raises problems[281] in the light of the large number of passages in which Jesus speaks of the futureness of the Kingdom, it is hardly likely to have been a creation of the early Church.   Not only did Jesus exorcise demons but this incident shows that others in Palestine at this time were doing the same: Jesus asks (v. 19), "If I cast out demons by Beelzebul, by whom do your sons cast them out?"   This argument would have been ineffective unless his opponents had to acknowledge the excorcisms by their own disciples.[282]   Jesus does not question that reality, but sees in their exorcisms as well as his own the evidence of God's Spirit powerfully at work.[283]

There can be little doubt that throughout Jesus' ministry in Galilee he spoke to his disciples and others about the ongoing struggle with supernatural forms of evil in which he and all God's people were and would be engaged.[284]   When victory is spoken of it is not so much Jesus' victory but, as this incident shows, that of God's Spirit (cf. Lk. 11:20; Mt. 12:28)—if the stronger one in Mk. 3:27 and parallels refers to Jesus, then it can only be Jesus as empowered by the Spirit, as the context clearly indicates.[285]   In the striking passage in Luke 10:18 (very Semitic and paralleled perhaps in John 12:31, also very Semitic) the *agent* of this victory over Satan is not specified, nor is it clear at which point in Jesus' Galilean ministry it is to be understood as having happened.[286]

The close connection between this activity of the Holy Spirit and the presence of the long-awaited Kingdom of God should not be surprising. Renewed evidence of the Spirit's working was expected to occur in the Age to come and this Spirit would be poured out broadly upon God's people, cf. e.g. Joel 3:1ff. (LXX 2:28f.).[287]

Similarly when Jesus replies to John's questioning doubts from prison (Lk. 7:18-23; Mt. 11:2-6),[288] he points to the miracles[289] he is performing (Lk. 7:21f.) as confirming the fulfillment of the dawn of the New Age that John had been proclaiming. Both John's emphasis on the coming cataclysmic judgment and Jesus' emphasis here on the wonderful qualities of the New Age are found in the Old Testament. Jesus is merely pointing John to another aspect of that eschatological reality (cf. e.g. Is. 11:6-9; 58:6-9; as well as the passages alluded to here in Q—Is. 35:5f.; 29:18f.). His final words to John: "Blessed is he whoever is not made to stumble by what he sees me doing" (v. 23) are an indication that Jesus does not see himself as the agent of God's cataclysmic judgment, as John had expected.[290] Similarly in the Lukan account of Jesus' rejection in his home village Nazareth (4:16ff.) Jesus declares that with his miracles (v. 18) and his proclamation of the good news of the Kingdom, the Messianic period has arrived: "Today, as you listen, these words are being fulfilled" (v. 21).[291] Finally, in the important passage in Luke 17:20,21 Jesus' reply to the Pharisees'[292] question when the Kingdom would come indicates that it is already here, in their midst, among them (*entos*)[293] (Lk. 17:21).

This passage, however, may indicate a further development in Jesus' thinking about the Kingdom, for in his reply he says that it comes not with observation, observable signs, so that one can say 'here it is' or 'there it is' (Luke 17:20f.). How is this to be understood in the light of Jesus' pointing to exorcisms and miracles as evidence of the Kingdom's arrival? Since Jesus has been proclaiming the arrival of the Kingdom, not only would John, the Pharisees, Jesus' own disciples be ultimately disappointed because the radical changes expected in the world in the New Age have not happened; but Jesus himself would have had to reconsider whether it had really arrived or not.[294]

It is in this connection that Jesus' frequent references to the Kingdom as *hidden* are best understood—while Jesus is still convinced it has arrived, as noted above, he can only conclude that its presence is hidden, and so looks forward once more to a *future* coming of the Kingdom '*in power*' (Mk. 9:1). This means *the actual situation has led Jesus to revise his world view once again*—whether he held one similar to the apocalyptic view of John and the Old Testament or, as is more probable, had an apocalyptic view similar to 1 Enoch.[295] Neither of these world views would fit with the realities of the world as it appears now that the Kingdom has arrived. Thus he seems to have come to a unique understanding of how God's plans for the Kingdom are being worked out. In his adjusted view the 'Messianic' age has begun, but *the shift of the Ages* has not occurred; instead of a radical removal of all sinners and evil, God's will appears to be that sin and evil remain in the world until some later point when God would bring about the cataclysmic world judgment and the radical transformation of the world and human existence in the New Age. Thus Jesus speaks of "this time" and "the Coming Age" (Mk. 10:30; Lk. 22:30).[296]

The difference between Jesus' new understanding and his earlier ones can be seen in the diagrams below:

Jesus' Earlier Views

a. Like John's View

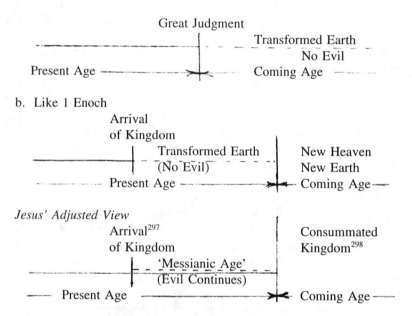

b. Like 1 Enoch

Jesus' Adjusted View

Mark 10:29f. raises an interesting point in this connection. In this passage Jesus promises the disciples who forsake all for the Kingdom that they will receive "now *in this time* a hundredfold, *houses* and brothers and sisters and mothers and children and *lands*,... and in the Age to come eternal life" (v. 30). This reference to houses and fields in the present time could only make the listeners think Jesus was speaking of a glorious life on earth in the Kingdom.[299] It is surprising that the early Church would retain such a statement in the tradition.[300] Both Matthew (19:29) and Luke (18:30) omit this very specific materialistic promise of rewards in the present Age. It may well be that it was statements like this which encouraged the early disciples to anticipate that Jesus would somehow establish or rule in an earthly Messianic Kingdom and that theirs would be special status and positions with him—cf. e.g. the request for special places by James and John (Mark 10:35ff.) and the surprising request of the earliest Christians to the resurrected Jesus "Lord will you at this time restore the Kingdom to Israel (Acts 1:6)?"

As Jesus waits for the consummation of the Kingdom which has already arrived, but remains largely hidden, he teaches about the nature of the Kingdom and those who come to share in it.[301] Often he does this with 'parables' which must be understood, however, in the broader sense of Hebrew *mashal* or Aramaic *mathla*.[302]

While some of the 'parables' clearly belong in a later period of Jesus' ministry (e.g. those which speak of irrevocable judgment, such as Mk. 12:1-11; Matt. 21:28-32; Luke 13:24-30); those which speak in more general terms of the Kingdom or of its hiddeness fit best in this period. One of the most instructive stories is that of the wheat and the weeds (Mt. 13:24-30). This is doubly attested, occurring also in the Gospel of Thomas (no. 57) and is considered by Crossan to go back to the historical Jesus.[303] This 'parable' shows clearly the adjustment Jesus has had to make concerning the presence of the Kingdom in view of the continuation of evil in the world and that he looks to the future for the eradication of evil, the cataclysmic judgment and the consummation of all things. This view is radically different than that of John the Baptist and best explains the Baptist's uncertainty about Jesus and provides a reasonable stimulus for John's question from prison.[304] 'Parables' which speak of the smallness of the Kingdom, its growth, the difficulty of recognizing and of saying "yes" to it would, it appears, fit into this period of Jesus' understanding of and teaching about the Kingdom.

Also characteristic of Jesus' teaching and ministry in this period may be his emphases on trusting the Father; on prayer; on giving precedence to human need over ceremonial and ritual requirements, a forgiving nature. If the parable of the barren fig tree in Luke 13:6-9 goes back to the historical Jesus,[305] it may well describe how he considered his role as he and all Israel wait for the full manifestation and consummation of the Kingdom—namely, to warn them that the time for recognition of and saying "yes" to the Kingdom is limited.[306]

Jesus' emphasis on prayer grows out of his own personal experience of dependence on the Father. The story in Mark 1:35-39 is particularly instructive here.[307] As Jesus plans to widen his ministry (vv. 38f.), he evidently seeks guidance and power through an extended period of prayer. This, no doubt, was his practice at various critical junctures in his life. It is in this way that his earlier solitude at the time of his baptism is to be understood, as well as other references to solitude and/or prayer (e.g. Mark 3:7, 13; 6:31, 46; 9:2). That this prayer life of Jesus grew out of his own sense of need and dependence on the Father is clear from his two parables about persistent prayer (the helpless widow Lk. 18:1ff. and the desperate friend Lk. 11:5ff.).[308] Particularly as Jesus seeks to understand the Father's plans concerning the Kingdom and his own role in it, Jesus would have been impelled to pray, especially that the Kingdom might soon come (cf. Lk. 11:2; Mt. 6:10).

It is in this period that the rift between Jesus and the religious leaders grows wider and more confrontative. Their antagonism against Jesus was not immediate—they (the Sadducees and Pharisees) were in Judea/Jerusalem,[309] whereas Jesus' prominent public activity was in Galilee. Prior to 70 C.E. the synagogues were autonomous and in Galilee their leadership would have been scribes and elders, with only a loose tie to the Jerusalem religious authorities.[310]

While many of the stories show the Pharisees in conflict with Jesus, the Pharisees may only later in Jesus' ministry have become interested in him enough to come from Jerusalem to Galilee to investigate him. A number of the accounts either mention only the scribes or scribes in conjunction with the Pharisees and/or the chief priests and elders.[311] It may be that, at first, Jesus' activity in Galilee came to the attention of the scribes and synagogue officials there and they then initiate with Jerusalem authorities their concerns. The mere fact of Jesus imperfectly following the laws of clean/unclean similar to the practice of the 'am-ha-aretz, would hardly have brought him to the attention of the Jerusalem leadership, nor warranted Galilean authorities to single him out.

Two factors may have resulted, however, in his eventual notoriety: his increasing popularity as crowds follow him; and his message that the Kingdom had arrived, as evidenced by his exorcisms and miracles.

Thus the traditions uniformly show masses of people coming to hear him and following him around—both for his message concerning the nearness/arrival of the Kingdom and also because of the message of hope, forgiveness and acceptance he offered them as being able to share in the Kingdom, in contrast to the scribes who, Jesus said, "do not enter themselves and seek to prevent others from entering." (Lk. 11:52; Matt. 23:13).[312]

Why would the Pharisees be opposed to John the Baptist's and Jesus' Kingdom proclamation? They were not adverse to the Kingdom as such. They too were looking forward to its coming, but not by human efforts to overthrow Rome and re-establish the Kingdom to Israel. They were looking for the day when *God* would do this. The religious leadership both in Galilee and Jerusalem were aware of the tendency of such Kingdom expectations to turn political. Neither they, nor Herod Antipas, nor the Romans were eager for this to happen.[313]   It is, perhaps, in this context that the Galilean religious leadership alerted the Pharisees to the popularity and activities of John's successor causing them to send representatives to investigate Jesus.

In a number of stories there is little or no antagonism evident on the part of either the Pharisees or Jesus.[314] Mark 2:15-17 can be understood as a sincere interest on the part of Jesus to encourage the religious leaders to recognize their own responsibilities as religious leaders to show concern similar to his own for the groups they despised. Mark 2:18ff. need not be anything more than a discussion concerning the practice of fasting and when it is appropriate. It implies that John has been removed from the scene and may indicate either his imprisonment, or his death.   Similarly Mark 2:23-28 appears to be a legitimate disagreement of what kind of activity can be allowed on the Sabbath. In the process Jesus claims *human need* takes precedence over ritual requirements.[315]   Sharpened criticism and antagonism is seen in the initial story (2:1-12) in this pre-Markan complex (2:1-3:6) where Jesus is accused of blasphemy, and in its concluding comment (3:6) that the Pharisees conspire with the Herodians to get rid of Jesus.   This difference between the individual stories in the complex reflects that they come from different periods in Jesus' ministry and have been joined together here (already in the pre-Gospel period) to form an explanatory introduction to the primitive pre-Markan passion account. Mark has taken the complex into his Gospel and used it as part of his structure, showing how all groups, the religious leaders (Mark 2 and 3), Jesus' family (3:20f.) have hardened themselves against Jesus (Mark 4:10-12); and how even the disciples themselves fail to recognize Jesus' real nature and task (Chaps. 5-8).

At some point in this period of great popularity Jesus becomes convinced that the public manifestation and consummation of the Kingdom is about to occur and thus sends out bands of his followers to declare its imminent manifestation.[316] What may have caused this decision on the part of Jesus? It could, of course, have been no more than a Spirit-worked perception, though this is nowhere hinted at in the sources. What is striking, however, is that the death of John the Baptist is mentioned in this context (Mk. 6:14-29; Lk. 9:7-9).[317] It may well be that Jesus saw in the death of John the Baptist, God's chosen messenger of the Kingdom, the climax of the opposition to God's plans and therefore urgently sends out his followers with a last-chance warning, which, if refused, is to result in total rejection of those people: "But whenever you enter a town and they do not receive you, go into its streets and say, 'Even the dust of your town that clings to our feet, we wipe off against you; nevertheless know this, that the Kingdom of God has come near'. I tell you, it will be more tolerable on that day for Sodom than for that town." (Lk. 10:10-12; Mt. 10:14, 15; Mk. 6:11).[318] The consequences for Jesus of both the death of John and the results of this mission will be examined in the next chapter.

Chapter 5

Jesus' Final Trip to Jerusalem

There is little doubt, as Crossan indicates, that the death of John the Baptist had great significance for Jesus and his understanding of the coming of God's reign.[319] There is no evident reason for the death of John to be recalled in the narrative about Jesus; and none of the Evangelists makes any explicit use of this reality,[320] in sharp contrast to their earlier use of John's imprisonment as a beginning point for Jesus' activity in Galilee.[321] Thus it must have come to them as a part of earlier traditions. Since the early Church had problems with a continuing Baptist movement, the extended inclusion of John's martyr-like death is all the more remarkable.[322] While there is no more certainty about the sequence of events here than there is elsewhere in the Gospels, it is significant also that all the Evangelists connect John's death with the sending out of the disciples and the miraculous feeding—Mark and Matthew have it follow the mission tour (Mk. 6:14; Mt. 14:1), Luke places it between his use of the Markan tour material (9:1ff.) and the Q version of the tour (10:3ff.); John does not have an account of the mission tour, but like the Synoptics places John's death (5:35) before and in close proximity to the miraculous feeding (chap. 6). This close connection of these 3 items—John's death, the mission tour and the miraculous feeding—evidently came to the Gospel writers as a part of their traditions.[323] A further indication of the early traditional sequence are the frequently noted[324] parallel sequences of Mark 6-7 and Mk. 8, as well as the close correspondence of these with the sequence of events narrated in John 6. It is striking that in this connection the Synoptics show Jesus three times withdrawing from the crowds and also from the disciples, often explicitly stated to be for the purpose of prayer (Mk. 6:31, 45f.; 8:10,13; retained in Mt. 14:13, 23; 15:21; Lk.

51

9:10,18).[325] In this is preserved a recollection of the critical nature of these events for Jesus himself as he seeks to learn from the Father what he is to do.

One possible interpretation of the significance for Jesus is perhaps indicated in the unique comment in the Matthean account that the disciples will not have "gone through all the towns of Israel *before the Son of Man comes*" (10:23). Neither the Markan nor Q form of this missionary tour in Luke contains this statement. It is hard to imagine why Matthew would add it to the tradition, since it is obviously incorrect; conversely it is easy to see why Luke would omit it from his form of Q, because of Luke's de-emphasis in his Gospel of the nearness of the End.[326] A further difficulty for the Church in Matthew's day would have been the limitation of the proclamation in this passage to the *Jewish* population of Palestine. This stands in sharp contrast to the world-wide mission responsibility indicated later in Matt. 28:19.[327]

A sense of urgency is evident in the various traditions and thus it appears that Jesus now looks forward to the *imminent* public manifestation of the Kingdom, an idea reiterated by Jesus in Mark 9:1: "Most assuredly I tell you that some of you who stand here will not experience death until they see the Kingdom of God has come *in power*."[328]

The Consummation of the Kingdom Is Imminent

What led Jesus to come to the conclusion that the final consummation of God's Kingdom was about to become manifest? While there can be no certainty, the death of God's chosen instrument, John, may well have caused Jesus to come to that conclusion. In any case around this time, it appears, it is with great urgency Jesus sends out groups of followers to give each village and town in Israel a last chance to say "yes" to the Kingdom before it is too late. That he thought of this as their *final* opportunity seems clear from the symbolic act of shaking off the dust of one's sandals as a testimony against them and their rejection of God's plan (cf. Mk. 6:11 and the Q forms in Lk. 10:11; Mt. 10:14) as well as the declaration of the terrible fate (worse than that of Sodom) which is found in Q (Lk. 10:12; Mt. 10:15).[329]

The initial result of this Kingdom proclamation seems to have been a large increase in the followers of Jesus. Thus soon after the disciples return the Gospels narrate the miraculous feeding (5000/4000).[330] This large increase in popularity would no doubt be partly due to Jesus' and the disciples' proclamation of the imminent appearance of the Kingdom and also the ministry of exorcism and miracles; but it could only awaken concern in the Roman and religious authorities that such popularity would lead to political unrest, as Brown posits: "The ministry of miracles in Galilee culminating in the multiplication... aroused a popular fervor that created a danger of an uprising..."[331] John's account includes the brief notice that the crowd's response at this time was "to come and take him by force to make him king" (6:15).[332] Some such response of the crowd as reported here must have occurred at some point in Jesus' ministry and is best understood as at least one of "the reasons behind the inscription on the cross (king of the Jews), and for Jesus quickly receiving the designation 'Christ' [Messiah] following the crucifixion and resurrection."[333]

The Delay[334] of the Consummation

In spite of the glowing reports of the disciples upon the completion of the tour (Lk. 10:17) and the increased following among the people there is a surprising undertone of disappointment[335] which is suggested by Jesus' response "come away by yourselves to a lonely place" (Mk. 6:30; Lk. 10:17; Mt. 14:13a). There is no reason for Mark to have added this to the tradition since, as Anderson notes, "so little does he [Mark] make of its significance that in what follows it is as if it never happened."[336] Such disappointment would not be surprising, since Jesus' prediction that the end would come before they finish their tour is not fulfilled.

From this point on, more than at any other time in his ministry perhaps, Jesus had to come to grips with his role and the nature of his leadership in the Kingdom. It is again striking that both John and the Synoptics show Jesus in dialogue with his disciples concerning this very issue (Jn. 6:67-69; Mk. 8:27-30)[337] and that in both the disciples declare him to be the Messiah (Jn. 6:69; Mk. 8:29). Jesus' response in the Synoptics is sharp and surprising—Peter is rebuked for the confession of Jesus as Messiah and told not to speak about this to anyone. While this command to silence is generally understood to be the Church's way of handling the largely non-Messianic nature of the traditions about Jesus whom they confess as Messiah,[338] there is no reason that it may not have come from Jesus himself as he seeks, *at this point*, to avoid the political revolutionary connotations of the term Messiah.[339] If Jesus does, *at this point*, reject such a title that may well account for both the Johannine notice of a large defection from Jesus[340] and the loss of popularity implied by Synoptic passages like Mark 10:23-31,32; Lk. 9:51-62; 10:2; 11:29; 18:8; Mt. 7:13f.; 11:18f. It is not surprising that when the Kingdom does not become manifest after Jesus had declared so prominently that it would occur before the end of the mission tour— not surprising that Jesus would lose much of his popular following.

Thus this complex of mission tour, miraculous feeding, discussion with his disciples of his special role in the Kingdom, death of John, coupled with unpopularity soon thereafter is best understood as Beasley-Murray and others note, as "one of the turning points in his ministry."[341] It is in this context that the Synoptic tradition recounts the transfiguration experience.

Jesus' Resolve to Proclaim the Imminence of the Kingdom in Jerusalem

Certainly for the Church in all its stages the significance of the transfiguration would be an epiphany of the divine nature of Jesus, of which they became convinced as a result of the resurrection. But the traditional material added by Luke to his account (9:31-33a)[342] indicates a different significance, and that for Jesus himself. The added Lukan material alone gives the *content* of the conversation: Moses and Elijah "appeared in glory and spoke of his departure, which he was to accomplish at Jerusalem" (v. 31). There is no way to determine what specifically took place as Jesus prays alone on the mountain.[343] The Lukan form, however, clearly intends to express Jesus' coming to the conviction that he must go to Jerusalem and there confront the religious center of Israel with the message of the imminent arrival of the consummation of the Kingdom. That he comes to a firm conviction on this point and realizes the serious consequences it may entail for him is clearly indicated in the subsequent Lukan notice "he set his face like flint to go up to Jerusalem" (9:51) which has a parallel in Mark 10:32: "And they were on the way to Jerusalem and Jesus was going ahead of them and they were amazed and the ones who were following were afraid."[344] John 11:16 also reflects the disciples' awareness of the seriousness of the danger when Thomas responds to Jesus' decision to go on this last trip to Jerusalem: "Let us also go that we may die with him."

It is most likely that it was subsequent to this "transfiguration" experience that Jesus began to speak to his disciples of the possibility of his suffering and even death in Jerusalem,[345] convinced that this too was part of God's plans for the consummation of the Kingdom.

That Jesus had anticipated the possibility of his suffering and even dying in Jerusalem, and that he had spoken of this to his disciples is not surprising.[346] He could not help but recognize the growing antagonism of the religious leaders who have begun to seek him out and challenge him even in Galilee.

While the threefold recounting of the passion prediction in Mark is clearly artificial and symbolic, it is significant that the first one (Mk. 8:31-9:1) is translation Greek.[347] Particularly it might appear that the statement "after three days" he would rise could only be a post-Easter addition of the Church. This is not likely since it does not agree with the fact that Jesus arose *on* the third day; and this 'correction' is made by both the Matthew and Luke accounts here (Mt. 16:21; Lk. 9:22) and also in the subsequent occurrences (Mt. 17:23; 20:19; Lk. 18:33. Lk. 9:44 omits the phrase). Rather, this is best understood as the symbolic use of the number 3, *indicating the complete or appropriate time span* (in the Father's determination). Similar symbolic use is found in reference to Jesus' ministry in Galilee (Lk. 13:32f.); the rebuilding of the temple (Mk. 14:58) and the 3 days and 3 nights of the sign of Jonah (Mt. 12:40)—which is even more incorrect with reference to the actual days and nights between burial and resurrection. There is no doubt that Jesus, like most Jews at this time, believed the Pharisaic doctrine of a general resurrection (cf. e.g. Mk. 12:18-27).[348]

In addition there are other passages which show Jesus having an awareness of and speaking about his death.[349] The conclusion of the pre-Markan complex 2:1-3:6 introduces the antagonism of the Jerusalem authorities too early, but eventually such opposition does develop because of Jesus' life and teachings and does become evident to Jesus. Jesus' reference to his death as a baptism which greatly distresses him (Lk. 12:50), as Kümmel points out, "so sharply contradicts the primitive Christian view of Jesus' way to death that we can hardly doubt that this saying belongs to the earliest Jesus tradition."[350] Behind Luke 13:33 ("it cannot be that a prophet should perish away from Jerusalem") there "lies a traditional belief about the fate of various prophetic figures in the city of Jerusalem,"[351] which Jesus uses here to interpret the necessity of this final trip.[352] As Jeremias correctly concludes: "This is not to argue that each of the many passion sayings is pre-Easter (every individual instance has to be examined). Nevertheless, we must note the total result that there can be no doubt that Jesus expected and announced his suffering and death."[353]

This awareness was a gradual development;[354] further, this possible outcome was not only passively acknowledged and accepted, but as Schweizer says: "What can be said on the strength of the real evidence is that at any rate Jesus did *nothing* to escape a violent death. On the contrary, despite the growing certainty that his message had, broadly speaking, been rejected, he *deliberately* [italics added] made for Jerusalem."[355] This does not mean that he went there "*in order* to die; but he did pursue with inflexible devotion, a way of truth that inevitably led him to death, and he did not seek to escape."[356] Thus the question that now needs addressing is how did Jesus look at his own death which he viewed as probable, if not inevitable? And why in Jerusalem? There can be no doubt that in some sense he saw it as intimately a part of God's plan and will for himself.

There are some indications in the Gospels of how Jesus viewed Jerusalem. The parable in Lk. 13:6-9, the barren fig tree, is particularly significant because it may indicate how Jesus himself[357] dealt with the non-arrival of the consummation of the Kingdom—the delay means God is giving *Jerusalem* one last chance, even though there is little hope for it. The two incidents (13:1-5) which Jesus mentions right before this parable both speak of catastrophes in Jerusalem (only there could sacrifices be offered) and end with the warning: Repent or perish similarly! If this is how Jesus interpreted the non-arrival of the Kingdom in its fullness, he may have felt called personally to go there and offer them this last chance to repent. If, however, he had been there previously and proclaimed the Kingdom as Lk. 13:34 suggests,[358] Jesus' purpose in going to Jerusalem now might be to declare to the Jerusalem hierarchy that the time for repentance has passed and only judgment awaits them. Passages like Lk. 19:41ff.[359] in which Jesus weeps over the city, as well as the sad lament in Q (Lk. 13:34f.; Mt. 23:37ff.) seem to express just such a hopeless situation and irrevocable judgment. In either case it is soon evident that nearly all of the Jesus material preserved in the Gospels and associated with this final stage of Jesus' life in Jerusalem shows Jesus in sharp confrontation with the religious leaders and often pronouncing harsh condemnation on them and inevitable destruction of the city.[360]

A third possibility is that Jesus goes to Jerusalem at this Passover, expecting that during this feast God would finally bring in the consummation of the Kingdom and thus vindicate his and the John the Baptist's proclamation.[361] Schweizer asks: "Did Jesus simply allow the certainty of his death to take possession of him in uncomprehending, though radical trust in God; or did he come to see in this historical situation some sort of divine plan of salvation, that not only in spite of but perhaps through the very failure within history of his message, through his death, his message would be vindicated divinely and in sovereign freedom?"[362] Related to this is the possibility that Jesus looked at his death as that of a martyr,[363] dying in a cause which God would ultimately validate.   He may even have considered his confronting of the religious establishment in Jerusalem as essential in a predetermined sequence of events which must transpire before God would finally bring in the Kingdom. In all of this one thing, at least, is clear—Jesus went to Jerusalem knowing that his death there was a very real possibility.

Jesus' Entry into Jerusalem

This is one of the few events which John's Gospel has in common with the Synoptics. Although Barrett and others consider John to have had one of the Synoptics before him as he wrote,[364] it is more generally agreed that John is independent of the Synoptics.[365] Thus the event is multiply attested and, in Mark, translation Greek.[366]   There is considerable disagreement over the significance of this event for Jesus. It is improbable that this was no more than an ordinary entry[367] at the time of Passover, which only in the handing on of the traditions comes to be molded and shaped into what appears in all the Gospels as a dramatic event. If this were the case, such modification must have happened at a very early stage[368] in the traditions for John and Mark (who is the source of Matthew and Luke) to agree in giving it such importance.

There are two details in the Markan account which suggests that Jesus in some sense deliberately arranged[369] for this entrance to be somewhat striking. *All four Gospels show Jesus taking the initiative in securing the animal*—in the Synoptics Jesus directs the disciples to the place where they would find a donkey[370] for him to ride on; John's Gospel merely says: "having found a young donkey, Jesus sat on it." There is no indication that this was his usual practice and could only attract attention since he alone of his group was riding.[371] The strange directions for securing the animal in the Synoptics suggest prior arrangement;[372] and even more so does the absolute use of "the Master" (*kurios*) in the disciples' explanation to the owner. While in later stages of the tradition *kurios* becomes a unique and exalted title for Jesus, during the lifetime of Jesus himself it would have been (in Aramaic) the natural way disciples would address their respected teacher. Why should the owner[373] be satisfied with such a reply? Only because he himself in some sense was a follower of Jesus and had agreed ahead of time to such an arrangement.[374]

Nor should it be disregarded that the *traditions agree in associating this event in close proximity to the Passover.* While all three major festivals drew crowds to Jerusalem with heightened expectations that God would in connection with such religious celebrations act to deliver his people, such hopes and fervor were particularly evident at Passover time.[375] Josephus indicates that the Roman Legate came to Jerusalem from Syria at such times and greatly increased the number of Roman troops stationed in Jerusalem compelling the Jews to "carry on their celebration under the watchful eyes of the Roman security forces stationed on the temple porticoes during such festivals."[376] For Jesus to come to the festival in this somewhat unusual manner could only raise nationalistic expectations in both his disciples and other festival pilgrims from Galilee.[377] It seems unlikely that Jesus would have been unaware of the nationalistic hopes which would be raised by his coming to Jerusalem in such a different manner at Passover It may well be asked: What did Jesus intend by such an act?

The traditions in the passion accounts of the Gospels contain indications of two things which Jesus may have been seeking to demonstrate by this strange arrival in the city, as well as by other things he said during this final week: First of all, he seeks to make clear that what he was convinced of since his baptism is still his firm conviction—namely, that he does have a special role in God's Kingdom; and second, that the term/concept "Messiah" concerning which there is much popular speculation in connection with himself, does not need necessarily to involve political revolutionary action.

Jesus Claims to Have a Special Role in the Kingdom

The first evidence of this as part of Jesus' *intention* is the fact (doubly attested in the Synoptics and John) that Jesus himself arranges for (Synoptics) or secures (John) the animal. There is no reason why both lines of tradition should agree in adding this detail to the account—evidently this is a recollection found in the earlier common tradition available to them.

In two passages (Mk. 11:27ff.; 12:1-9 and pars.) Jesus indicates that any rejection of him is the same as rejecting the Kingdom he proclaims. This debate with the religious leaders of Jerusalem is one of the most significant evidences that Jesus realizes he has a special role in relation to the Kingdom. That it goes back to Jesus himself is most probable,[378] though a number of scholars ascribe it to the early Church.[379] It is, however, unlikely, as Mann also notes, that the early Church would "build the authority of Jesus on that of John."[380] The fact on which Jesus bases his query in this account is that the religious leaders in Jerusalem had rejected John's baptism and message, yet the ordinary people accepted both (cf. Lk. 7:29f.; Mt. 21:32).[381] Jesus says in effect, since you rejected John, you have rejected also God's Kingdom; similarly your rejection of me is likewise a rejection of God's Kingdom,[382] for both of us are God's messengers of the Kingdom's coming.

In the parable in Mk. 12:1-9 Jesus makes the same point. There is general agreement that the parable is authentic,[383] but less agreement on what Jesus meant by it. Its application, however, in the sense that rejection of the messenger is a rejection of the One who sent the messenger seems beyond dispute and applies equally to John, Jesus and any others in their role as spokesmen for God.

A striking way of speaking on Jesus' part makes its appearance in the traditions associated in the Gospels with this later period of his ministry—in a few instances both Jesus and others refer to the Kingdom with 1st or 2nd person personal pronouns, indicating that in some sense it is Jesus' Kingdom! In Mark 10:37-40 James and John ask Jesus for places of dominance in his glory. The context indicates glory here probably refers to places of power in the Kingdom[384] Jesus has been discussing with them. While some consider this to be Mark's editorializing in order to show these disciples in a negative light, Funk (although his group does not consider the account authentic) notes: "A

story of two prominent disciples attempting to grab power is not likely
to have been invented after the crucifixion" and he indicates that the
group's judgment was divided in this matter.[385]   Taylor finds the
incident "in every way credible."[386]   A similar situation and usage is
preserved by Luke in 22:29,30 where Jesus promises he will give them
a Kingdom, just as the Father, Jesus says, has given "me a Kingdom in
order that you may eat and drink at *my* table in *my* Kingdom."[387] The
thief on the cross asks Jesus, "Remember me when you come into *your*
Kingdom" (Lk. 23:42). Fitzmyer cautiously accepts the possibility that
such an exchange actually took place, noting little evidence of Lukan
redaction in the account and suggests that the thief may have been led
to ask this because of the accusation Pilate had posted on Jesus'
cross.[388] The crucifixion of Jesus by the Romans as a rebel Jewish king
implies he claimed in some sense to have a kingdom; and in the
independent Johannine scene before Pilate (18:36) Jesus says "*my*
Kingdom is not of this world."   The infrequency of this kind of
language in the Gospels, as well as its occurrence in a number of
different settings, literary forms and sources indicates Jesus' thinking of
himself as having a special role in the Kingdom is to be understood as
a recollection in the traditions, rather than a redactional element of the
Gospel writers.

Finally, Jesus' conception of his special role in the Kingdom is
indicated in some sense when he speaks of "*my* blood of the covenant"
in Mark 14:24 in connection with the wine of the Last Supper. While
there is no agreement on the specific meaning of the phrase, this
Markan text reflects the earliest form of the word spoken in relation to
the cup and by its very awkwardness betrays its Aramaic origin.[389]

The Term Messiah Does Not Necessarily Involve Political Revolutionary Action

While the dominant popular connotation of the term Messiah was of
a Davidic leader who would forcefully remove foreign domination from
Israel,[390] the term could be associated with other meanings as well. One
way to understand Jesus' intentions here is that he wanted, by this
manner of entry, to lead the people to a non-revolutionary understanding
of the term.[391]

First it should be noted that a variety of people seem to consider
Jesus to be the nationalistic Davidic military leader/king who was to

come.[392] This is no doubt the view of the crowds who enthusiastically hail him as the "Son of David" (Matt. 21:9), "the King who comes in the name of the Lord" (Lk. 19:38), "King of Israel" (John 12:13); "Blessed is he who comes in the name of the Lord! Blessed is the kingdom of our father David which is coming" (Mk. 11:9f.).

Further, the Roman officials in Palestine were particularly cautious of nationalistic "messianic" movements[393] and since this is the official category under which Jesus was crucified (cf. the charge attached to the cross "the King of the Jews"), it is clear that they understood Jesus to have made some sort of claim to this title. Similarly whatever other charges the religious leadership in Jerusalem would press against Jesus, they apparently made their appeal to Pilate on the grounds that Jesus was making some sort of nationalistic messianic claim.

Also among the disciples there is evidence that some of Jesus' followers looked to him in terms of nationalistic messianic hopes—the most obvious example is the name of one of them—Simon the Zealot (Lk. 6:15).[394] Two other indications of such nationalistic expectations among the disciples in Luke's writings are Acts 1:6 where the disciples ask the resurrected Jesus: "Lord, are you now going to restore the kingdom to Israel?" and the translation Greek[395] account of the two disciples on the road to Emmaus (Lk. 24:13-35). In this account the two disciples are in despair since they had looked to Jesus as "the one who would deliver Israel" (v. 21). Clearly this Emmaus account is a pre-Lukan, Palestinian tradition.[396]

The implication of Jesus' rejection of Peter's confession that he is the Messiah in Mk. 8:27-30 is that Jesus, at least, understood it to be a nationalistic political concept[397] which had connotations he was not willing to encourage.

One final passage may imply political revolutionary expectations—Lk. 22:35-38.[398] Jesus' comment here (that 2 swords are sufficient) is best understood as being ironic[399] and may indicate his awareness that against his earlier teachings some of the disciples expect sharing in possible violent conflict to bring in the Kingdom.[400]

There are some indications that Jesus himself may have anticipated ruling in an earthly messianic Kingdom. One of the most striking indications is his response to Peter that anyone who has left all to follow him will "receive a hundredfold now in this time *houses* and brothers and sisters and mothers and children and *lands*..." (Mk. 10:29f.). It is improbable that the Church would have added such crassly materialistic details.[401] The promise that the disciples would sit on thrones judging Israel (Lk. 10:30; Mt. 19:28) as well as Jesus indicating the Father alone assigns places of honor next to Jesus (Mk. 10:40) clearly imply Jesus' expectation of ruling in a Kingdom; but whether it is to be so in his lifetime is unclear.

It is over against such expectations, which Jesus himself may have earlier deliberately or unintentionally suggested, that Jesus with this final approach to Jerusalem seeks to demonstrate more clearly that *he has no aspiration to be a revolutionary political deliverer.*

If Jesus held to the basically quietistic expectations of the Scribes and Pharisees[402] who, while they await a Davidic Messianic ruler, do not expect that Davidic leader to bring in the Kingdom of God by armed revolution—rather expecting God himself to deliver the nation and to establish the Davidic ruler on the throne—then Jesus may only be seeking to demonstrate a non-violent role in the Kingdom for himself.

This would agree with his earlier criticism that "from the days of John the Baptist until now [John's imprisonment] the kingdom of heaven has suffered violence and men of violence take it by force" (Mt. 11:12), clearly rejecting violence in his own proclamation of the Kingdom. As noted above his ironic rejection of two swords (Lk. 22:35ff.) would carry the same message and it has been suggested, so would also his choice to enter Jerusalem on a donkey, rather than a horse, followed by a small unarmed group of disciples.[403] The fact that later in Passover week the crowds reject Jesus as a political deliverer (Mk. 15:8ff. and pars.; Jn. 18:40) and their choice of Barabbas, a known revolutionary (Lk. 23:19), which is independently attested in Mark (15:6-15) and John (18:39f.), confirm this interpretation of the crowd's rejection of Jesus.

The most striking evidence, however, may be Jesus' dialogue with the Pharisees in Jerusalem concerning the lineage of the Messiah (Mk. 12:35-37). This passage most probably reflects an authentic dialogue between Jesus and religious authorities[404] since in it Jesus appears to deny, or at least cast doubt on the Davidic lineage of the Messiah, one of the prime tenets of the early Church![405]

The *meaning* of this exchange is hotly debated, more concerning its significance in Jesus' own day rather than how it was understood in later Christian use.[406] Fitzmyer lists three possible meanings in the case of Jesus:[407] "(a) Jesus is calling in question the Davidic origin of the

Messiah... (b) Many ancient and modern commentators have understood the question of Jesus to imply that the Messiah is to be something more than a mere son of David, one having a more exalted or transcendent origin than David... (c) Some interpreters have pressed beyond the second interpretation to specify that Jesus would have been referring to himself as the Son of Man of Dan. 7:9-13." While most scholars reject the first possibility,[408] a number accept it and see Jesus in this exchange rejecting either the entire concept of a Davidic Messiah or seeking to reinterpret it in non-revolutionary, non-political terms.[409]

Kümmel notes "the tradition does not tell us how Jesus personally related to being addressed as 'Son of David' [e.g. Mk. 10:47f.] and we are lacking any indication that Jesus ever stressed his Davidic ancestry."[410] There is no doubt that the later Church did stress the Davidic lineage of Jesus, but it must be remembered that the traditions also surprisingly give Jesus a priestly lineage[411] through Mary. There are two ways to interpret Mark 12:35ff. which are related to the Messianic expectations of the Essenes.

The Messianic expectations of the Essenes are better known now because of the discoveries at Qumran. There were at least 3 eschatological figures in the Qumran expectations: 1) an "eschatological prophet" 2) "a high priestly Messiah" 3) "a lay head of the eschatological community (the Annointed One of Israel)."[412]

There has been some debate whether Qumran expected *two* Messiahs or not, since the phrase "the Messiah(s) of Levi and of Judah" is enigmatic.[413] If there were actually 2 such Messiahs expected, the priestly Messiah is clearly dominant and the one of Judah subordinate, even as in Qumran administration the priestly element dominated. Warlike activity was associated with the Messiah of Judah. Jesus may have had this type of Essene understanding in his background, both because of his own genealogy, as well as because of possible influence of the Essenes/Qumran and their ideas through his earlier association with John the Baptist and with this dialogue he may have intended to reject for himself the warlike Messiah they expected.

However, in the Damascus Document the term Messiah is *singular*[414] and in that connection Charles[415] has made an interesting observation which suggests a second possible way of understanding Jesus' meaning in Mark 12:35ff. Charles notes that the phrase is "The Messiah (sing.) from Aaron and Israel." Thus, he concludes, the Messiah according to this document will have mixed lineage, partly Levitic and partly non-

Levitic. This is, Charles suggests, a reference to the descendants of Herod through Mariamne, since Mariamne was Levitic on both her parents' sides and Herod was a non-Levitic (half) Jew, i.e., descended "from Israel." Charles proposed that the writer of the document "may have cherished the hope that one of them[416] might become the Messiah, just as similar hopes had arisen in connexion with the earlier Macccabees in the second century B.C."[417] Charles, further, notes specifically the antagonism in this document to the Davidic line and thus explains the more general designation "and from *Israel*" rather than "from David."[418] In the light of this possibility the genealogical traditions of Jesus (Levitic on his mother's side and Davidic on his stepfather Joseph's side) would make the apparent denigration of a purely Davidic Messiah in the argumentation used by Jesus in Mark 12:35f. even more understandable.

In whatever way, then, the Essene expectation is to be understood, Mark 12:35f. may be a further indication that Jesus is seeking to direct attention away from the nationalistic revolutionary aspects of the Messiah, but at the same time does not reject his own special role as ruler/leader in the consummation of the Messianic kingdom which he expects in the very near future, even while he is in Jerusalem at this Passover festival.[419]

While it appears Jesus enters Jerusalem hoping that God would during this festival bring about the consummation of the Kingdom, he seems to become more and more uncertain that this will happen before his death.[420] Three aspects of this last week's activity reflect Jesus' inner turmoil in this matter: 1) his strange arrangements concerning the securing of a room for (what he assumes) will be his last Passover meal with his disciples; 2) his struggle in prayer in Gethsemane to accept what he sees as God's will, even though it may be different and less desirable than his own expectations; 3) his cry of abandonment on the cross (Mk. 15:34).

Jesus' Strange Arrangements concerning the Room for Passover

First of all it must be remembered that Jesus evidently was particularly concerned to be able to eat this Passover with his disciples (as Luke 22:15 "with desire I have desired to eat this Passover with you" shows). Since he knows he is at great risk during this visit to Jerusalem,[421] it is not surprising that he would make special arrangements for the place where he will share with them this meal, which he feels may well be his final meal.

A number of details in the Markan account (Mk. 14:12-17)[422] are best understood in this light.[423] First of all there is some surprise shown by the question of the disciples (v. 12) that so far, on the very day preparations must be made for the meal, they know nothing of the arrangements. Instead of a simple, straight forward answer Jesus chooses two disciples and gives them very round-about directions on how to locate the room where the meal is to be eaten. The question naturally arises why such strange directions? It is clear that none of the other disciples know where the meal is to be eaten until later that evening Jesus brings them to the house. Thus it appears Jesus sends two trusted disciples[424] on the task and gives them instructions in the hearing of the rest which will be of no help to any of them in learning the location of the house ahead of time.[425] It is more probable that the directions concerning the man carrying water reveals pre-arrangement (as other details will confirm) than that Jesus has foreknowledge in this matter or that a writer has arbitrarily composed the narrative in this peculiar manner.[426]

The message these two disciples are to convey is indeed striking. First of all, the use of "The Teacher" suggests this is a person who would thereby recognize that these are sent by Jesus[427] and is himself one of Jesus' followers in a broad sense. Secondly, Jesus speaks of "*my* guest room"[428]—this surely fits best with Jesus having followers in Jerusalem where he has stayed from time to time. There may have been more than one such place. As noted earlier it is most probable during his ministry (before and after John's imprisonment) that he has visited Jerusalem at least during the 3 main pilgrimage festivals each year and would have contacts there.[429] The fact that the room is already prepared for Passover, then, is completely understandable, leaving the two disciples only with the task of obtaining the lamb from the Temple and cooking it. The details of this passage fit well with the evidence of Jesus' initiative and pre-arrangement in connection with the entry into the city earlier.[430] There the arrangements were to call attention to himself and his role; here they are to secure privacy for the final meal.

Jesus' Struggle in Prayer in Gethsemane

While there can be little doubt that the Markan wording of Jesus praying the Garden is hardly a verbatim record, the likelihood of his spending these final moments before his anticipated arrest in prayer is most probable.[431]   The tradition is doubly attested (Mk. 14:32-42; Hebrews 5:7) or even triply so if either the Matthean account (translation Greek!)[432] or the Lukan reflects the use of non-Markan traditions.[433]

Jesus' prayers at this point should probably be understood as a final attempt to learn whether the Father will bring in the Kingdom before his death, which reality appears most imminent to him now.[434] Whether the Father will choose to do so or not, is not made known to Jesus, evidently, and from this point onwards Jesus must live these last hours not knowing what the Father plans, but willingly accepting whatever the Father's will is for him in respect to the Kingdom. This acceptance is symbolized by the *threefold* praying, which is most probably editorial, symbolically representing the substance of a tradition that Jesus ultimately resolves to follow whatever path his subsequent experiences will show to be the path the Father chooses for him.[435]   Another indication of Jesus reaffirming at this time the Father's control of events is the statement in Matthew at the time of his arrest (26:53) that if he so requested, the Father could send "more than twelve legions of angels" to rescue him.   Matthew here is translation Greek[436] and receives independent support by the Johannine statement of Jesus to Pilate that he has not sought by force of arms to avoid arrest (18:36). All of this does not mean that Jesus has given up the hope that the Father will yet bring in the Kingdom before he dies; rather, that Jesus now leaves the entire matter in the Father's hands.

Jesus' Cry of Abandonment on the Cross

No word of Jesus in the Gospels reflects Jesus' complete humanness[437] more than this cry of abandonment in Mark 15:34. It is inconceivable, as Taylor noted, that the "tradition would have assigned to Jesus such a saying except under the warrant of the best testimony. Its offence is manifest in the silence of Luke and John and in the textual tradition."[438]

Attempts have been made to soften this cry of dereliction by claiming that although only the opening phrase of Ps. 22 is cited, this is intended to call to mind the entire Psalm[439] and thus must be understood as a statement of complete trust, as is found in the final verses of the Psalm (vv. 22-31). Taylor rightly rejects this, considering it to be "a reaction from the traditional view which fails to take the saying seriously."[440]

This cry of Jesus is only an *allusion* to Psalm 22, not a direct quotation— since the Markan Aramaic does not agree either with the extant Targum of Psalm 22, nor with the Hebrew text of the Psalm. The Markan Aramaic disagrees with the Targum in having *elōi* instead of *'ēli* and *lama* instead of *metūl mā*.[441] Rather than being a literary citation of the first line of Ps. 22 (to indicate the entire Psalm) this distinctive non-Targumic Aramaic of Jesus here testifies to its authenticity as a word of Jesus drawn from his inmost being as he faces imminent death and has, it appears, no awareness of the Father's presence which has sustained him throughout his life up to these final moments.[442]

Does this cry mean that Jesus no longer trusts the Father? Hardly, he has already struggled through to acceptance of whatever the Father chooses. This is more an expression of horror at not being able in this critical time to experience the Father's nearness nor to understand even at this last moment the Father's purposes. Whether the Lukan words of trust in the Father in these last moments (Lk. 23:46) are authentic or not, they do cohere with how Jesus has lived his entire life up to this point and may well express the willingness to trust even when understanding is not given.[443] The assurance the dying Jesus gives to the thief on the cross ("assuredly I tell you today you will be with me in Paradise" Lk. 23:43) also coheres with the life-long trust of Jesus, his view of life after death, and his conviction, as expressed in the last meal with his disciples, that he will drink wine with them in the Kingdom—whether or not his conversation with the thief reflects an actual incident. It coheres also with Jesus' uncertainty as to whether the Kingdom is to come before or after his death, convinced in either case that it is extremely imminent. In other words, even as Jesus dies, not understanding why and not being able to *experience* the sustaining support of the Father, he dies absolutely confident in the Father whom he has learned to trust throughout his entire life.[444]

Efforts to interpret Jesus' own understanding of the significance of his death, on the basis of titles such as Son of Man, Son of God, Servant, etc., are not likely to succeed because already in the earliest post-crucifixion period the Church[445] sought to use a variety of such titles to express the significance of the cross. More than other traditions, it appears that the titles are too enshrouded with later meanings to be helpful in seeking to understand how *Jesus* interpreted the significance of his death, even though one or more of them in all probability have some grounding in Jesus' own statements.

The title which most clearly must be associated with Jesus during his lifetime is the term Messiah.[446] It is the title under which he dies[447] and is, as far as can be determined, the earliest confession of the earliest Christians. How could they come to the absolute conviction that this Jesus who died the death of a criminal and revolutionary on the cross was indeed God's promised Messianic deliverer? The answer to that will be sought in the Epilogue below.

Epilogue

Any study of Jesus as he was and what he said and did during his lifetime must somehow come to grips with the question of how the historical Jesus as recovered by critical study is to be related to the Jesus whom the earliest disciples and followers come to confess as God's promised Messiah and Deliverer.[448]

The traditions preserved in the Gospels and Acts show that this confession was not the earliest Christians' immediate and automatic response. Rather, surprisingly, the traditions show the disciples to be confused, fearful and uncertain because of the horrible death of Jesus.[449]

The traditions preserved indicate two things which altered all of this—the resurrection of Jesus and the outpouring of the Holy Spirit. All of the accounts of the empty tomb and of the appearances of the resurrected Jesus in the Gospels are second and third hand reports.[450] There is, however, one *first hand* report of an appearance of the risen Jesus—that of Paul the Pharisee.[451] As noted in an earlier study of Paul:[452]

> It is, indeed, striking that such a traditional, well-trained, scrupulously-following-Torah Pharisee, who violently persecutes those who proclaim Jesus as God's promised Messiah—striking that *such* a person should change and join them in proclaiming Jesus' Messiahship! What could have effected such a change? Paul says: no one human did this; God accomplished it—and that by an encounter with the risen Jesus himself.

Paul had this experience very early in the 30's and it was this event, he says, which enabled him to accept that Jesus who had been crucified as a criminal/revolutionary was indeed God's Messiah.[453] This event also began a process in which Paul reorients his entire thinking about eschatology, as well as the place of Torah and the Gentiles in the Messianic Age which he now knows has arrived.[454]

His own experience of the risen Jesus evidently also enabled Paul to accept the early Christian tradition that hundreds of people had seen Jesus after his resurrection.   Paul hands this tradition on to the Corinthians in 1 Cor. 15:3-8: "For I handed on to you as of first importance what I in turn had received: that Christ died for our sins in accordance with the Scriptures, and that he was raised on the third day in accordance with the Scriptures, and that he appeared to Cephas, then to the twelve. Then he appeared to more than five hundred brothers at one time, *most of whom are still alive,* though some have died. Then he appeared to James, then to all the apostles. Last of all, as to one untimely born, he appeared also to me."

The changes which Paul had to make in his thinking as the result of his own experience of the risen Jesus are typical, no doubt, of the changes which each of the earliest followers of Jesus had to make when they saw the risen Jesus or otherwise became convinced that he was, indeed, the Messiah God had promised to send. This conviction became their earliest confession—first in Aramaic: Jesus (is) the Messiah; and then in Greek: Jesus (is) the Christ.[455] This confession which appeared essentially as "Jesus, the Messiah" becomes a *title* for Jesus. Eventually Messiah (Christ) became a part of *Jesus' proper name.* Paul in the late 40's and 50's reflects this transition from title to proper name, at times using it one way and then the other.[456]

Both Paul (e.g. Gal. 3:2f.—written ca 50 C.E.)[457] and Acts (written ca 85-90 C.E.) indicate, further, that it was the Holy Spirit which accomplished this radical change in the understanding of Jesus in the lives of the earliest Christians; just as the Church has confessed down through the ages that the acceptance of Jesus as God's promised Messiah and Deliverer is still the accomplishment of the *Spirit's* working.

Both Paul and the early Church in general had to make the same eschatological adjustments which Jesus had made in his lifetime—while the Messianic Age had, indeed, begun, *the shift of the Ages* (bringing in the New Age and the consummation of all things) had not yet happened.   There are two discernible adjustments which the early Christians made—one in the period 30-70 C.E.; the other after the devastation of Jerusalem in 70 C.E.

30-70 C.E.

In this period Christians confess that the Messiah has come and they are certain that they are living in the period just before the imminent arrival of the eagerly awaited consummation of all things. This is particularly evident from statements by Paul in which he reveals his own eschatological expectations (ca 45-55 C.E.).

While Paul is convinced the Messianic Age has begun, he speaks in Gal. 1:4 of "the present evil Age" and in Rom. 8:18-23 of the "groaning of all creation" and also of Christians who "have the first fruits of the Spirit" but "wait eagerly for the revealing of the sons of God;" for, he says (in Phil. 3:20f.) "our commonwealth is in heaven, and from it we await a Savior, the Lord Jesus Christ, who will change our body to be like his glorious body." This final transformation at the return of Messiah Jesus Paul expects to happen very soon, before he dies (1 Thess. 4:13ff.; 1 Cor. 15:51f.).[458] This view can be diagrammed as follows:[459]

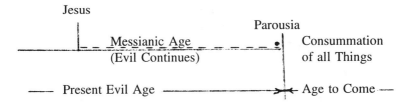

Mark (ca 65-70 C.E.) writing in close proximity to the devastation of Jerusalem reflects a similar position, as is evident in the way he handles the traditions he has received (e.g. Mark 13). His view is very similar to Paul's:

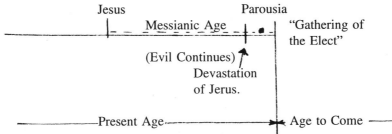

After 70 C.E.

Luke's Gospel reflects a further adjustment the writer and his generation of Christians had to make because the Parousia still had not come. By his redaction of Mark and other traditions, while he is certain that the Messianic Age had begun in Jesus (Lk. 4:16ff.), Luke pushes the final consummation of all things into the indefinite, more distant future. This is shown by the changes he makes in Mark's 'Little Apocalypse' (Lk. 21:5ff., esp. v. 9 "the end [is] not yet/at once").

Luke's view has in effect become the view which the Christian community has had to live with for some 2000 years; it can be diagrammed as follows:

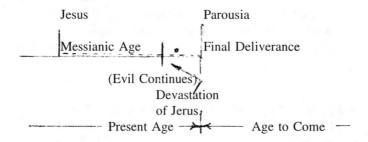

Just as Jesus in his human condition had to trust the Father in the midst of uncertainty concerning the time of the End of all things (Mk. 13:32), those who followed had to learn to do the same.

Appendix 1

Syntax Criticism of *Q* Material

The following chart indicates those units in Q which are clearly translation Greek in either Matthew or Luke or both according to the 17 syntactical criteria of translation Greek isolated by syntax criticism.[460] The listing clearly shows that these syntactical features are not equally distributed throughout the Q source, and that the distribution is not necessarily the same in Matthew and Luke. Further these features appear in all three layers as isolated by Kloppenborg. *This inconsistency of distribution throughout Q material and throughout Matthew's and Luke's separate forms of Q* shows that these Semitic features cannot be due to the Greek writer's natural Semitized Greek style or be the result of familiarity with LXX Greek, but reflect instead those units of tradition which in the process of transmission have had clear evidence of their previous Semitic, Palestinian milieu preserved.[461]

Along with other frequently cited criteria Kloppenborg analyzes a number of *syntactical* features whose frequency or infrequency has been considered evidence of translation Greek. In doing this he dealt with the *totals for Q as a whole* and concludes that there is no convincing evidence of translation.[462] If the frequencies of the three criteria of syntax criticism he uses are analyzed in *individual sections* of Q, however, the translation Greek character of parts of Q become very evident,[463] as the chart on page 75 shows.

73

The 21 Translation Greek Sections of Q[464]

	Translation Greek	Original Greek	Ambiguous
Sapiential Q			
4 Love for Enemies (A)	Lk 6:27-31		Mt 5:39-42;7:12
5 Love for Enemies (B)	Lk 6:32-36		
	Mt 5:43-48		
6 Judging Others (A)	Lk 6;37,38,41,42		Mt 7:1-5
14 Woe to Cities	Lk 10:13-15		Mt 11:21-23
15 Jesus Rejoices	Lk 10:21-24		
	Mt 11:25-27;13:16		
16 Lord's Prayer	Mt 6:9-13		Lk 11:2-4
17 Teaching About Prayer	Lk 11:9-13		
	Mt 7:7-11		
23 Warnings	Lk 12:2-9		
	Mt 10:26-33		
25 Care and Anxiety (B)	Lk 12:33,34		
	Mt 6:19-21		
31 Banquet Parable	Lk 14:15-24	Mt 22:1ff.	
32 Cost of Discipleship	Lk 14:26,27		Mt 10:37,38
Apocalyptic Q			
10 Centurion's Servant	Mt 8:5-13	Lk 7:1-10	
11 John's Messengers (A)	Lk 7:18-23		Mt 11:2-6
19 Demand for a Sign	Lk 11:29-32		
	Mt 12:39-42		
20 The Light of the Body	Lk 11:33-35		
	Mt 5:15;6:22f.		
21 Denunciation of Pharisees (A)	Lk 11:39-44		Mt 23:23-27
22 Denunciation of Pharisees (B)	Lk 11:45-51		
	Mt 23:4,29-36		
27 Concerning Watchfulness	Lk 12:42-46		Mt 24:45-51
Introduction to Q			
2 Temptation of Jesus	Lk 4:1-13	Mt 4:1-11	
Other Q Sections			
33 Lost Sheep Parable	Lk 15:4-7		Mt 18:12-14
36 Parable of Pounds	Lk 19:11-27	Mt 25:14-30	

Syntactical Feature	Kloppenborg[465]	Martin[466]		
	All of Q	All of Q	Transl. Q	Rest of Q
Kai:De (Translation Greek = 2.1 + KAI for each DE)[467] Luke's Q Matthew's Q	1.6:1 2.1:1	2.3 (136:59) 2.3 (130:57)	3.1 (92:30) 3.4 (44:13)	1.5 (44:29) 2.0 (86:44)
Separation of Article (Translation Greek = .05-Separated)[468] Luke's Q Matthew's Q	8.37% 9.19%	.07(457:32) .10 (459:45)	.05 (287:13) .01 (132:1)	.11 (170:19) .13 (327:44)
No. of Attr. Adj. Preceding for Each One Which Follows (Translation Greek = .35-Preceding)[469] Luke's Q Matthew's Q	4.0 (12:3) 2.0 (16:8)	.54 (13:24) .63 (22:35)	.29 (4:14) .13 (1:8)	.90 (9:10) .78 (21:27)

The conclusion arrived at by syntax criticism as to whether a document is or contains translation Greek is not based so much on the frequencies of *individual* criteria as it is on the *cumulative net frequencies* (i.e. the number of original Greek frequencies which occur compared to the number of translation Greek frequencies.)[470] When the net frequencies of these 17 criteria for the 21 translation Greek sections of Q are compared to the net frequencies of the rest of the Q sections, the difference is striking, as the chart on the following page shows.

It appears that while Matthew and Luke had very similar if not identical copies of *Greek* Q, they each in their own way retained or improved on the Semitic Greek features of their text and these modifications along with other editorial activity cause sometimes Matthew and more often Luke to appear as translation Greek when the other does not. In this matter, then, their editorial work on Q is quite similar to the editorial activity they reveal when dealing with their common Markan text—with the qualification that the Greek text of Q which they had was in general more Semitized than their Greek text of Mark. Thus the Q sections in both Matthew and Luke still evidence a more pronounced Semitic syntactical quality than Mark does.[471]

Finally, the above 21 sections are the *minimum* of translation in Q. Of the 36 units in Q *only one* (24. Care and Anxiety A) has clear original Greek frequencies in both Matthew and Luke![472] Fourteen units fall into the area of ambiguity (i.e. that area shared by both original Greek and translated Greek)[473] in Matthew or Luke or both—i.e. 39% of the Q material. In the initial study the amount of *undetected translation of known translated documents* was found to be as high as up to 54% (the quite idiomatic LXX translation of Genesis) or 58% (the LXX translation of the Aramaic sections of Daniel). The average undetected for all the control translation Greek documents was 37%.[474] Thus it appears probable that all, or nearly all, of the Q material had an Aramaic background before it made its appearance in Greek.

In the light of the foregoing discussion the diagram which follows on page 78 may suggest how both the Greek and Semitic features of the Q material in Matthew and Luke may be accounted for.

Net Frequencies in Original Greek Documents of More Than 50 Lines in Length

	NO. OF LINES	NET NO. OF FREQUENCIES CHARACTERISTIC OF ORIGINAL GREEK																	0	NET NO. OF FREQUENCIES CHARACTERISTIC OF TRANSLATION GREEK													
		17	16	15	14	13	12	11	10	9	8	7	6	5	4	3	2	1	0	-1	-2	-3	-4	-5	-6	-7	-8	-9	-10	-11	-12	-13	-14
PLUTARCH - SELECTIONS	325		x																														
POLYBIUS - BKS I,II	192			x																													
EPICTETUS - BKS III,IV	138	x																															
BKS I,II	349									x																							
BKS I,II,III,IV	487							x																									
JOSEPHUS - SELECTIONS	215		x																														
PAPYRI - SELECTIONS	630	x																															
II MACCABEES 2:13-6:31	495	x																															
PHILO - ON CREATION I-VIII	251									x																							
HEBREWS	535		x																														
ACTS 15:36-28:31	1056		x																														
LUKAN Q																																	
CLEARLY TRANSL.	243								x																			x					
REST OF LUKE Q	148																						x										
TOTAL LUKE Q	391																																
MATTHEAN Q																																	
CLEARLY TRANSL.	109																			x													
REST OF MATT. Q	258													x														x					
TOTAL MATT. Q	367																																

Net Frequencies in Translated Documents of More Than 50 Lines in Length

Document	No. of Lines	Net No. of Frequencies Characteristic of Original Greek																	0	Net No. of Frequencies Characteristic of Translation Greek													
		17	16	15	14	13	12	11	10	9	8	7	6	5	4	3	2	1		-1	-2	-3	-4	-5	-6	-7	-8	-9	-10	-11	-12	-13	-14
GENESIS 1-4,6,39	382														x																		
I SAMUEL 3,4,22	194																													x			
I KINGS 17	58												x																				
2 KINGS 13	71																														x		
DAN. -HEBREW - LXX	482																												x				
-HEBREW - THEOD.	460																													x		
DAN. -ARAMAIC - LXX	595																													x	x	
-ARAMAIC - THEOD.	634																															x	x
EZRA -HEBREW	328																																
-ARAMAIC	211																													x			
JER. -PROSE A (CHAPS 1,3,7,11,16)	201																												x				x
-POETIC A (CHAPS 2,4,5,6,10)	357																																x
JER. -PROSE B (CHAPS 33-36)	216																										x						
-POETIC B (CHAPS 30,31,37,38)	171																										x						
EZEK.-PROSE A (CHAPS 2-5)	200																																x
-POETIC A (CHAPS 19,27)	74																													x			
EZEK. -PROSE B (CHAPS 28,30-32)	203																															x	
-POETIC B (CHAPS 33-35)	132																													x			
I MACCABEES (CHAPS 1-5)	732																														x		

The percentages and numerical counts on which these net frequencies are based are found at the end of this appendix.

Tradition History of Q

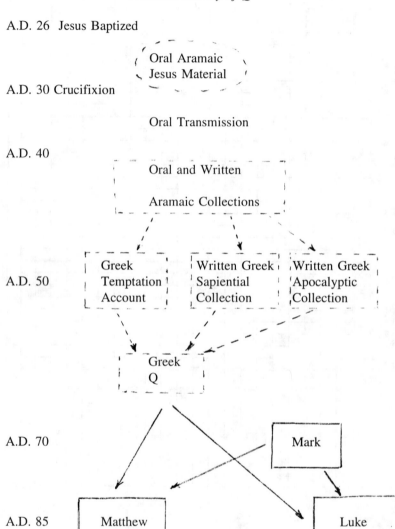

A.D. 26 Jesus Baptized

Oral Aramaic
Jesus Material

A.D. 30 Crucifixion

Oral Transmission

A.D. 40

Oral and Written

Aramaic Collections

Greek
Temptation
Account

Written Greek
Sapiential
Collection

Written Greek
Apocalyptic
Collection

A.D. 50

Greek
Q

A.D. 70   Mark

A.D. 85   Matthew   Luke

Net Frequencies of Lukan and Matthean Q Material

Translation Frequencies	No. of lines of Greek text	No. of occur. of en	dia W. gen. (.06-.01)	dia W. all cases (.18-.01)	eis (.49-.01)	kata W. accus. (.18-.01)	kata W. all cases (.19-.01)	Peri w. all cases (.27-.07)	Pros w. dative (.024-.01)	Hupo w. genitive (.07-.01)	No. of occur. of kai for each occur. of de (2.1+)	Percent. of separ. articles (.05-)	No. of dep. gen. post/ea. prec. dep. gen. (22+)	No. of lines/ea. dep. gen. pers. pronoun (9-)	Lines/ea. dep. pers. pron. on anarth. subst. (77-)	No. of prec. attr. adj. for each attr. adj. post position (.35-)	No. lines/ea. attrib. adjec. (10.1+)	No. of lines/each adverb. participle (6+)	No. of dat. not used w. en for ea. occur. (2-)	Tot. no. of transl. Grk. frequencies (17)	Tot. no. of orig. Grk. frequencies	No. of inst. where occ. of criter. are too few to be indic.	Net original Grk. frequencies	Net translat. Grk. frequencies (17)
Lk Tr Alone	151	28	–	.11	.21	–	–	.07	–	.04	3.5	.05	8.7	4.6	151.0	.44	11.6	3.5	1.1	17	–	–		17
Lk (Mt.) Tr	92	11	–	.09	.36	–	–	–	–	.09	2.4	.04	38	5.4	92	.00	18.4	13.1	1.7	9	4	4		-5
All Tr Lk	243	39	–	.10	.26	–	.09	.05	–	.05	3.1	.05	15.0	4.9	243.0	.29	13.5	4.9	1.3	11	2	4		-9
All Non-Tr Lk	148	14	.07	.21	.86	.07	.03	.29	–	.21	1.5	.11	11.0	5.3	148	.90	7.8	4.0	2.5	11	3	3		-8
All Lk Q	391	53	.02	.13	.42	.02	.14	.11	–	.09	2.3	.07	13.2	5.0	391.0	.54	10.6	4.5	1.6	3	13	1	+10	
Mt Tr Alone	22	5	–	–	.40	–	–	–	–	–	6.0	.00	11.0	2.0	22.0	1.0	11.0	2.8	.80	7	3	7		-4
Mt (Lk) Tr	87	19	–	.05	.16	–	–	–	–	.05	2.9	.01	14.7	3.8	87	.00	12.4	43.5	.63	10	2	5		-8
All Tr Mt	109	24	–	.04	.21	–	–	–	–	.04	3.4	.01	13.8	3.2	109.0	.13	12.1	10.9	.67	10	3	5		-8
All Non-Tr Mt	258	30	.07	.13	.73	.03	.07	.10	–	.10	2.0	.13	15.3	4.1	258	.78	5.4	4.4	1.9	6	10	1	+4	
All Matt Q	367	54	.04	.09	.50	.02	.04	.06	–	.07	2.3	.10	14.7	3.8	367.0	.63	6.4	5.3	1.4	9	7	1		-2

Translation Greek Sections in Q - Numerical Summaries[1]

I. Q SECTIONS WHICH ARE TRANSLATION GREEK BOTH IN LUKE AND MATTHEW

A. THE LUKAN VERSION

	LINES	EN	DIA G	DIA T	KATA EIS	KATA A	KATA T	PERI T	PROS D	HUPO G	KAI	DE	ART. UNSEP	ART. SEP	DEP.GEN PREC	ART c GS DS	ART c GS DP	NO ART c GS DS	NO ART c GS DP	ATTR ADJ PREC	ATTR ADJ POST	ADVERBIAL PARTICIPLES	DATIVES
5. 6:32-36	12	-	-	-	-	-	-	-	-	-	4	-	11	-	-	-	3	1	-	-	-	1	4
15. 10:21-24	13	2	-	-	-	-	-	-	-	1	6	-	15	-	-	-	1	1	-	-	1	1	3
17. 11:9-13	9	-	-	-	-	-	-	-	-	-	7	1	9	1	-	-	1	-	-	-	2	1	3
19. 11:29-32	12	2	-	-	1	-	-	-	-	-	5	1	15	-	-	6	-	1	-	-	-	1	2
20. 11:33-35	6	1	-	-	1	-	-	-	-	-	-	1	12	1	-	1	4	-	-	-	-	1	-
22. 11:45-51	17	-	-	-	1	-	-	-	-	-	3	4	20	2	-	4	3	3	-	-	1	2	5
23. 12:2-9	18	5	-	-	1	-	-	-	-	-	3	5	21	-	-	4	2	-	-	-	-	-	1
25. 12:33,34	5	1	-	1	-	-	-	-	-	-	1	-	4	-	-	-	3	-	-	-	1	-	1
TOTALS	92	11	-	1	4	-	-	-	-	1	29	12	107	4	-	15	17	6	-	-	5	7	19

B. THE MATTHEAN VERSION

	LINES	EN	DIA G	DIA T	KATA EIS	KATA A	KATA T	PERI T	PROS D	HUPO G	KAI	DE	ART. UNSEP	ART. SEP	DEP.GEN PREC	ART c GS DS	ART c GS DP	NO ART c GS DS	NO ART c GS DP	ATTR ADJ PREC	ATTR ADJ POST	ADVERBIAL PARTICIPLES	DATIVES
5. 5:43-48	11	1	-	-	-	-	-	-	-	-	4	1	14	-	-	-	6	1	-	-	1	-	-
15. 11:25-27; 13:16,16	12	1	-	-	-	-	-	-	-	1	5	1	13	-	-	-	2	2	-	-	-	1	3
17. 7:7-11	8	1	-	-	1	-	-	-	-	-	5	-	9	-	1	-	3	-	-	-	1	1	3
19. 12:39-42	11	3	-	-	1	-	-	-	-	-	5	1	15	-	-	6	-	1	-	-	2	-	-
20. 5:15; 6:22,23	6	2	-	-	-	-	-	-	-	-	2	1	14	-	-	1	4	-	-	-	-	-	1
22. 23:4,29-36	17	3	-	-	1	-	-	-	-	-	5	2	21	-	1	7	3	2	-	-	3	-	3
23. 10:26-33	16	7	-	-	-	-	-	-	-	-	4	4	19	1	1	1	3	-	-	-	-	-	-
25. 6:19-21	6	1	-	1	-	-	-	-	-	-	2	1	3	-	-	-	2	-	-	-	-	-	2
TOTALS	87	19	-	1	3	-	-	-	-	1	32	11	108	1	3	15	23	6	-	-	7	2	12

[1]The numbers at the left margin refer to the numbering of these sections in the initial study in SC Syn G, pp. 91-95 and Appendix 4.

LINES	EN	DIA G	DIA T	KATA ES	KATA A	KATA T	PERI T	PROS D	HUPO G	KAI	DE	ART. UNSEP	ART. SEP	DEP-GEN PREC	ART. C GS DS	ART. C GS DP	NO ART. C GS DS	NO ART. C GS DP	ADJ PREC	ADJ POST	ADVERBIAL PARTICIPLES	DATIVES
II. ONLY MATTHEW Q TRANSLATION GREEK																						
10. 8:5-13 — 15	3	-	-	1	-	-	-	-	-	10	2	13	-	1	-	4	-	-	1	-	8	3
16. 8:5-13 — 7	2	-	-	1	-	-	-	-	-	2	-	10	-	-	-	6	-	1	-	1	-	1
TOTALS — 22	5	-	-	2	-	-	-	-	-	12	2	23	-	1	-	10	-	1	1	1	8	4
III. ONLY LUKE Q TRANSLATION GREEK																						
2. 4:1-13 — 19	4	-	-	1	-	-	1	-	1	10	3	20	-	1	2	1	3	-	-	1	6	2
4. 6:27-31 — 8	-	-	-	-	-	-	-	-	-	3	-	14	-	-	-	1	-	-	-	-	-	4
6. 6:37,38,41,42 — 12	5	-	1	1	-	-	-	-	-	7	2	17	3	-	2	7	-	-	1	-	3	2
11. 7:18-23 — 13	2	-	-	-	-	-	1	-	-	6	1	9	-	-	-	2	1	-	-	-	5	3
14. 10:13-15 — 5	4	-	-	-	-	-	-	-	-	1	1	3	-	-	-	3	-	-	-	1	1	7
21. 11:39-44 — 13	2	-	-	-	-	-	-	-	-	3	2	24	1	-	3	1	-	-	-	1	1	4
27. 12:42-46 — 12	4	-	-	-	-	-	-	-	-	4	1	18	1	-	1	6	-	-	-	1	2	2
31. 14:15-24 — 22	1	-	2	2	-	-	-	-	-	13	2	24	-	2	3	3	-	-	1	1	6	2
32. 14:26,27 — 5	-	-	-	-	-	-	-	-	-	-	-	8	-	2	-	-	3	-	-	-	-	-
33. 15:4-7 — 9	2	-	-	1	-	-	-	-	-	3	-	10	-	-	-	2	-	-	2	-	6	3
36. 19:11-27 — 33	4	-	-	1	-	-	-	-	-	13	6	20	4	1	1	6	-	1	-	4	13	3
TOTALS — 151	28	-	3	6	-	-	2	-	1	63	18	167	9	6	12	32	7	1	4	9	43	32

Translation Greek Sections in Q - Numerical Summaries

	LINES	EN	DIA G	DIA T	EIS	KATA A	KATA T	PERI T	PROS D	HUPO G	KAI	DE	ARTICLE UNSEP	ARTICLE SEP	DEP. GEN. PREC	ART. c GS DS	ART. c GS DP	NO ART. c GS DS	NO ART. c GS DP	ATTRIB. ADJ. PREC	ATTRIB. ADJ. POST	ADVERBIAL PARTICIPLES	DATIVES
IV. GROUP SUMMARIES																							
A. LUKE Q																							
LUKE ONLY TR.	151	28	-	3	6	-	-	2	-	1	63	18	167	9	6	12	32	7	1	4	9	43	32
WHEN MATT. ALSO TR.	92	11	-	1	4	-	1	-	-	1	29	12	107	4	-	15	17	6	-	-	5	7	19
ALL LUKE TR.	243	39	-	4	10	-	1	2	-	2	92	30	274	13	6	27	49	13	-	4	14	50	51
ALL LUKE NON-TR.	148	14	1	3	12	1	2	4	-	3	44	29	151	19	5	20	28	7	-	9	10	37	35
ALL LUKE Q	391	53	1	7	22	1	3	6	-	5	136	59	425	32	11	47	77	20	1	13	24	87	86
B. MATTHEW																							
MATT. ONLY TR.	22	5	-	-	2	-	-	-	-	-	12	2	23	-	1	-	10	-	1	1	1	9	4
WHEN LUKE ALSO TR.	87	19	-	1	3	-	-	-	-	1	32	11	108	1	3	15	23	6	-	-	7	2	12
ALL MATT. TR.	109	24	-	1	5	-	-	-	-	1	44	13	131	1	4	15	33	6	-	1	8	10	16
ALL MATT. NON-TR.	258	30	2	4	22	1	2	3	-	3	86	44	283	44	7	33	63	11	-	21	27	59	58
ALL MATT. Q	367	54	2	5	27	1	2	3	-	4	130	57	414	45	11	48	96	17	1	22	35	69	74

Appendix 2

Summary of Changes in Jesus' Eschatological Expectations

APPENDIX 2

SUMMARY OF CHANGES IN JESUS' ESCHATOLOGICAL EXPECTATIONS

1. The Kingdom is near
    Jesus in Judea as John's disciple
        (pp. 25-43)[475]

2. The Kingdom has arrived (pp. 43-45)
    Indicated by Jesus' exorcisms
    Jesus' Nazareth sermon (Lk. 4:16ff.)
    Jesus thinks the 'shift of the Ages'
    has occurred

3. The Kingdom is hidden and its consummation
        is future (pp. 45-50)
    Parable of wheat/weeds (Mt. 13:24ff.)
    John's question from Prison
        (Lk. 7:18ff./Mt. 11:2ff.)
    Luke 17:20
    Jesus' realizes the 'shift of the
        Ages' has not occurred

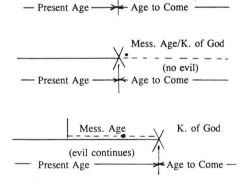

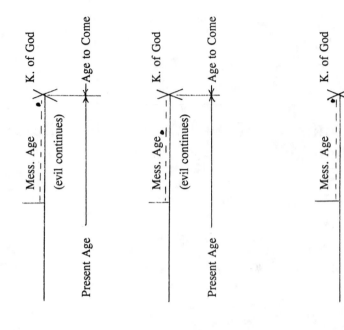

4. The consummation of the Kingdom
    is imminent (pp. 50-53)
    John the Baptist's death (Mk 6:14ff.)
    Disciples' preaching tour
        (Lk 6; Lk 9;10/Mt 10)
    Feeding 4000/5000 and great
    popularity (Mk 6;8)

5. The consummation of the Kingdom
    fails to occur (pp. 53-57)
    Crowds desert Jesus (Jn 6:66)
    Increased antagonism against Jesus
    Transfiguration (Lk. 9)
    Jesus discusses his death
    in Jerusalem (Mk 8;9)
    Jesus decides to make a final
    appeal/judgment in
    Jerusalem (Mk 10;32; Lk 9:51)

6. Final Days in Jerusalem awaiting
    the consummation of the Kingdom[476]
    (pp. 57-68)
    The Last Supper (Mk. 14:25)

Notes

1. *Jesus and Judaism* (1985), p. 2.

2. Cf. e.g. J.D. Crossan, *The Historical Jesus* (1991), p. xxvii; J.H. Charlesworth, *Jesus within Judaism* (1988), pp. 168f.

3. Cf. e.g. W. Kümmel, *Theology of the New Testament* (1973), p. 58.

4. Cf. e.g. E. Boring's listing of ten ["Criteria of Authenticity" in *Forum*, Vol. 1 (1985), pp. 3-38 with an extended bibliography (pp. 32-38)]; cf. R. H. Stein's eleven in "The 'Criteria' for Authenticity" in *Gospel Perspectives* (1980), Vol. 1, pp. 225-263; also articles in *Forum*, Vol. 5 (1989); R. Funk, *The Gospel of Mark (Red Letter Edition),* 1991, pp. 29-52.

5. J. Meier writes: "...one senses that the last forty years have produced a rough consensus on valid sources, method and criteria in that most enduring of treasure hunts, the quest for the historical Jesus. "Reflections on Jesus-of-History Research Today," *Jesus' Jewishness*, ed. by J. Charlesworth (1991), p. 85.

6. These are the traditions that have been passed on by the earliest followers of Jesus, many of whom would have been with him in the years preceding his death; also these traditions were in the language (Aramaic) commonly used by Jesus and his followers.

7. This was the earliest criterion used by those who initiated the new

quest for the historical Jesus. Cf. e.g. N. Perrin, *Rediscovering the Teaching of Jesus* (1967), pp. 39ff.

8. Stein notes it is also called "criterion of discontinuity" (*ibid.*, p. 242); E. Schillebeeckx: "dual irreducibility" and "distinctiveness." *Jesus* (1979), p. 92.

9. Cf. the criticisms of this criterion in H. McArthur, *In Search of the Historical Jesus* (1970), pp. 142ff.; Stein, *op. cit.*, pp. 241ff.; J. Jeremias, *New Testament Theology* (1971), p. 2; Schillebeekx, *op. cit.*, pp. 93ff.

10. *Op. cit.*, p. 98.

11. *Ibid.*, p. 99. Cf. e.g. also Stein, *op. cit.*, p. 235; Boring, *op. cit.*, p. 10.

12. So Schillebeeckx; *loc. cit.*; Stein, *loc. cit.*; this criteria is not mentioned or used in Funk, *op. cit.*

13. Schillebeeckx, *op. cit.*, pp. 98ff., *et al.* The authenticity/earliness of the *Greek* Palestinian traditions will need to be decided on the basis of other criteria than Aramaic, Palestine milieu data.

14. Cf. e.g. Schillebeeckx, *op cit.*, p. 99; earlier N. Turner, "The Relation of Luke I and II to Hebraic Sources and to the Rest of Luke-Acts," *New Testament Studies*, Vol. 2 (1955-56), pp. 100-109.

15. Cf. e.g. H. F. D. Sparks, "The Semitisms of St. Luke's Gospel," *Journal of Theological Studies*, Vol. 44 (1943). Cf. also P. Winter, "Two Notes on Luke I, II with Regard to the Theory of 'Imitation Hebraisms'" in *Studia Theologica*, Vol. 7 (1953), p. 165.

16. H. F. D. Sparks, "The Semitisms of Acts," *Journal of Theological Studies*, n.s. Vol. 1 (1950), p. 28.

17. H. Conzelmann, *Acts of the Apostles* in *Hermeneia* (1987), pp. xxxvf.

18. E. Haenchen, *Acts of the Apostles* (1971), pp. 75f.

19. J. Fitzmyer, *The Gospel according to Luke* (1981), Vol. 1, pp. 114, 116, 123.

20. Cf. studies by Raymond Martin: *Syntactical Evidence of Semitic Sources in Greek Documents* (1974)*(Syn Ev)*; *Syntax Criticism of the Synoptic Gospels* (1987)*(SC Syn G)*; *Syntax Criticism of Johannine Literature, the Catholic Epistles, and the Gospel Passion Accounts* (1989)*(SC Joh)*. The Semitic nature of each of the features used in the above studies was demonstrated in *Syn Ev*, pp. 5-38.

21. Cf. Winter, "Two Studies," p. 165; also Martin's earlier studies noted above where this was pointed out and illustrated.

22. For a fuller statement of this matter cf. *SC Syn G*, pp. 25-31 and *SC Joh*, pp. 174f.

23. Cf. the text and summary charts in *Syn Ev*, pp. 87-91 and the text and summary chart in *SC Syn G*, pp. 25-27.

24. Cf. Fitzmyer, *op. cit.*, p. 109. Cf. E. Schweizer, "Eine hebraisierende Sonderquelle des Lukas?" in *Theologische Literaturzeitung*, Vol. 6 (1950), pp. 162ff.

25. Cf. Martin, note 23, *supra*.

26. Cf. Chart VI "Classification of Material in Acts" in *SC Syn G*, pp. 32-36.

27. Cf. Martin, *ibid.*, Chaps. I, II, III; also pp. 128-130.

28. Cf. *SC Syn G*, p. 73 and the detailed analyses pp. 47-65. Cf. also Fitzmyer, *op. cit.*, p. 106: "One need only to consider Luke's wording and reformulation of the Marcan material to become aware of his concern to improve its Greek style."

29. Martin, *ibid.*, Chaps. I-III.

30. Cf. Schweizer also: "Wir setzen ein bei Lk., weil wir seinen Stil an Hand der Acta nachprüfen können. Sollten Formulierungen nachweisen sein, die im Evangelium häufig sind, in Act. fehlen, insbesonders im zweiten Teil, wo Lk. unabhängig von Quellen schreibt, so besteht eine ziemliche Warscheinlichkeit, dass sie nicht dem Lk., sondern einer von ihm verwerteten Quelle (oder mehreren) zugehören." "Eine hebraisierende Sonderquelle," pp. 162f.

31. Cf. *SC Joh*, pp. 1-4 and 5-42.

32. Cf. Raymond Brown, *The Gospel according to St. John.* (1966), Vol. 1, pp. xxxivf. He indicates that Stages 1 and 2 belong to the Aramaic level of Gospel traditions and that those of Stage 1 "may already represent ten or twenty years of development from the time of Jesus" (p. xlviii). He indicates that it was Stage 3 that saw "the organization of this material from Stage 2 into a consecutive Gospel. This would be the first edition of the Fourth Gospel as a distinct work... Most probably this first edition was in Greek and not in Aramaic" (p. xxxv). He writes later: "Personally, we tend to agree with the majority of scholars who do not find adequate evidence that a complete edition of the Gospel according to John (Stage 3) ever existed in Aramaic. It is possible, however, that bits of the historical tradition underlying John [Stages 1 and 2] were written in Aramaic..." (p. cxxx).

33. Cf. McArthur, *op. cit.*, p. 139. Schillerbeeckx calls it "the principle of cross-section" (*op. cit.*, p. 95).

34. Cf. e.g. Stein, *op. cit.*, p. 230; McArthur, *op. cit.*, p. 140.

35. Even though the MS of the Coptic Gospel of Thomas is dated in the 4th Christian century, fragments of the Greek text occur in Oxyrhynchus papyri dated paleographically to ca. 200 C.E. and scholars generally then date the original composition to ca. 140 C.E. It is generally conceded to be independent of the canonical Gospels. Cf. R. Cameron, "Thomas, Gospel of" in *Anchor Bible Dictionary, Vol. 1* (1992), pp. 535f.; J. Menard, "Thomas, Gospel of" in *Interpreter's Dictionary of the Bible. Supplement* (1976), pp. 902ff. R. Funk, *The Parables of Jesus* (Red Letter Edition), 1988, pp. 10f.

36. After a detailed survey of the issue of Johannine dependence on the Synoptic Gospels, Brown concludes: "To summarize, then, in most of the material narrated in both John and the Synoptics, we believe that the evidence does not favor Johannine dependence on the Synoptics or their sources. John drew on an independent source of tradition about Jesus, similar to the sources that underlie the Synoptics. *Op. cit.*, p. xlvii. Cf also R. Fortna, *The Gospel of Signs*, (1970), p. 227; E. Haenchen, *John* in *Hermeneia* (1984), Vol. 1, p. 90: "The Evangelist has not made use of any of the other three canonical gospels in his narrative segments, although respectable scholars like Kümmel and Hirsch are convinced of the contrary." C. K. Barrett also sees dependence on the Synoptics. *The Gospel according to John* (1978), p. 15.

37. "The Priority of Mark and the Q Source in Luke" in *Jesus and Man's Hope* (1970), pp. 131-170. Cf. also C. M. Tuckett, "Q (Gospel source)," *Anchor Bible Dictionary*, Vol. V (1992), p. 567; M. Boring, Review of Kloppenborg, *The Formation of Q* (1987) in *Journal of the American Academy of Religion*, Vol. 58 (1990), p. 293. Cf. Appendix 1 for a discussion of the Semitic sections of Q and a proposed tradition history of the Q source.

38. Cf. *SC Syn G*, pp. 37, 89.

39. *Op. cit.*, p. 95.

40. *Op. cit.*, p. 141.

41. Also called "coherence." Cf. Boring, "Criteria," p. 17.

42. Cf. Stein, *op. cit.*, pp. 249, 257.

43. *Op. cit.*, p. 96.

44. *Ibid.*, p. 97.

45. *Ibid.*

46. Cf. e.g. *ibid.*, p. 92; Stein, *op. cit.*, p. 252.

47. Kümmel, while noting the difficulties of getting back to the historical Jesus and the need for the use of all possible critical tools in the process, continues, "on the other hand it is also wrong to approach this task with the demand, often made in recent times, that the 'genuinness' of each individual word of Jesus and the historicality of every individual story must be proved. For there is no reason at all for the opinion that the historical reliability of a piece of tradition can only be an exception... Of course the decisive check on the correctness of such a setting apart of the earliest body of tradition can only be *the proof that from the fitting together of the pieces of tradition thus gained a historically comprehensible and unitary picture of Jesus and his proclamation results, which also makes the further development of primitive Christianity understandable* [italics added]." *Op. cit.*, p. 26.

48. Cf. Sanders, *op. cit.*, p. 11; Charlesworth, *op. cit.*, p. 169. Sanders suggests that initially a study of the historical Jesus should concentrate "primarily" on "facts about Jesus, his career, and its consequences which are very firm and which do point towards solutions of historical questions... and only secondarily on a study of some of the sayings material." *Ibid.*, p. 4.

49. The infancy stories in Luke and Matthew are clearly independent of one another. Cf. Fitzmyer: "When all is said and done, there is no reason to doubt that Jesus' birth took place in the days of Herod; this is independently attested." *Op. cit.*, p. 404.

50. Cf. G. Caird, "Chronology of the NT," *Interpreter's Dictionary of the Bible* (1962), Vol. 1, pp. 599f.; K. Donfried, "Chronology, New Testament," *Anchor Bible Dictionary* (1992), Vol. 1, p. 1012; R. E. Brown, *The Birth of the Messiah* (1979), p. 166.

51. Cf. Caird, *op. cit.*, p. 600.

52. Cf. e.g. D. Braund, "Archelaus," *Anchor Bible Dictionary* (1992), Vol. 1, pp. 367f. and S. Sandmel, "Archelaus," *Interpreter's Dictionary of the Bible* (1962), Vol. 1, p. 207. Other chronological details in Luke 2:1f. are either too broad (Caesar Augustus' rule) or evidently too confused (Quirinius' census) to be useful for dating Jesus' birth. Cf. Fitzmyer, *Luke 1*, pp. 393, and esp. 399-405; cf. also Caird,

op. cit,, pp. 600f.; Donfried, *op. cit.*, pp. 1012f.

53. Fitzmyer (*Luke 1*, p. 308). He writes: "The term would be more accurately used of the Matthean text than the Lucan, because Matthew at least quotes the OT, and a starting point in an OT text is an essential of Midrash. Even then it would have to be used only in the broadest of senses." *Ibid.*, pp. 308f.

54. Cf. Martin, *SC Syn G*, pp. 113-118, particularly no. 2, p. 114.

55. Fitzmyer notes that while in some sense midrash might be suitable as a description of the Matthean infancy narrative, "it is, in any case, quite unsuitable for the Lukan form." *Luke 1*, p. 309.

56. Cf. e.g. Fitzmyer, *op. cit.*, pp. 109, 113-127; I. Marshall, *The Gospel of Luke* (1979), pp. 46f.; Brown, *Birth*, p. 246.

57. Cf. N. Turner, *op. cit.*, pp. 100ff., particularly p. 109. Hardly anyone would adopt this view today and the analysis of Luke-Acts by syntax criticism demonstrates that Turner's view is untenable. Cf. *Syn Ev* and *SC Syn G passim*.

58. Cf. Sparks, *op. cit.*, p. 28. As noted in the Introduction (*supra*, pp. 2f.) this is the most widely held view today.

59. Cf. Marshall's listing of those who posit Hebrew and Aramaic sources. *Op. cit.*, p. 46; Brown, *Birth*, p. 246.

60. Brown defines the term source somewhat more narrowly. He writes: "In the discussion that follows I am using the term 'source' in a technical way: an oral or written consecutive narrative or collection of material." *Birth*, p. 241, n. 19.

61. Cf. e.g. Brown's discussion in *John 1*, pp. 236-239.

62. Brown sees a greater likelihood of sources in Luke (in his technical sense of the term noted *supra*, n. 60) "for explaining the composition of ch. 2." *Birth*, p. 247.

63. Cf. the data in Martin, *SC Syn G,* pp. 99f.

64. *Ibid.*

65. Cf. the listing in Brown, *Birth* (p. 246): Dibelius, Michaelis, Plummer, Spitta, B. Weiss, Box, Dalman, de Lagarde, Gunkel, Laurentin, Streeter, Torrey, Winter.

66. Fitzmyer: "In fact, it makes little difference to the interpretation of the Lucan Gospel whether or not one can establish that its author was the traditional Luke." *Luke 1,* p. 53.

67.   While not insisting that Luke is the author of Luke-Acts, Fitzmyer indicates that the traditions extant about Luke show that "the source of such [Semitic] interference [in his Greek] could be Luke's origin in Syrian Antioch, where he lived as an *incola,* speaking the Aramaic dialect of the indigenous natives of that country, though he was also educated in the good Hellenistic culture of that town. A Palestinian background of some material cannot be ruled out." *Ibid.,* p. 116.

68. Cf. Brown's comments. *Birth,* p. 246.

69. Cf. e.g. Marshall, *op. cit.,* pp. 48f.

70. Cf. Brown's discussion. (*Birth,* pp. 245). Fitzmyer (*Luke 1,* p. 308) rejects such speculation as "sheer conjecture." Acts 1:14 includes Jesus' mother and brothers in the small pre-Pentecost group of believers.

71. *Birth,* pp. 34f.

72. *Op. cit.,* p. 307.

73. *Ibid.,* pp. 306f.; similarly Brown, *Birth,* p. 34.

74. Cf. Epiphanius (d. 405 C.E.) who "besides stating that James was appointed bishop by the Lord... says that he was a priest and wore the 'petalon' (the ornament of the high priest's mitre, Ex. 28:36f.; 29:6)

and went once a year into the Holy of Holies (as if he were the officiating high priest)." J. Ropes, *The Epistle of St. James, International Critical Commentary* (1916), p. 72.

75. Cf. the synoptic listings in Brown, *Birth*, pp. 77-79 and Fitzmyer, *Luke 1*, pp.492-494.

76. *Ibid.*, pp. 494f.; cf. also Brown, *Birth*, pp. 84f.

77. *Ibid.*, pp. 495ff. Cf. also Brown, *ibid.*

78. Cf. Fitzmyer, *ibid.*, p. 500; also F. Gingrich, "Heli," *Interpreter's Dictionary of the Bible*, Vol. 2 (1962), p. 579.

79. Brown writes: "And the names Luke gives for the post exilic period reflect Levitic descent (e.g. Levi, Mattathias), a curious feature in a Davidic lineage." R. Brown "Genealogy (Christ)," *Interpreter's Dictionary of the Bible. Supplement* (1976), p. 354. It may be noted, further, that it is with the son of David named Nathan that Luke's list goes radically its own way. The Nathan of 1 Kings 4:5 is apparently of priestly lineage and may be the person actually intended in the pre-Lukan listing. Cf. S. Sziksai, "Nathan," *Interpreter's Dictionary of the Bible*, (1962), Vol. 3, p. 511.

80. "Genealogy," p. 354.

81. *Luke 1*, p. 491. B. Throckmorton agrees: "In conclusion it may be said that the genealogies were probably drawn up independently, quite early, by different Jewish Christians in the interest, primarily, of substantiating Jesus' messiahship." "Genealogy (Christ)," *Interpreter's Dictionary of the Bible*, Vol. 2 (1962), p. 366.

82. Suggested by Annius of Viterbo. Cf. Throckmorton, *op. cit.*, p. 366. He notes Lagrange's tracing of this view "back to the fifth century" and that in recent times it was defended by B. Weiss. Marshall notes also G. Kuhn (1923) as holding this view. *Op. cit.*, p. 159. Fitzmyer cites J. Heer also. *Luke 1*, p. 397.

83. So Brown, *Birth*, p. 89; Fitzmyer, *ibid.*; Marshall, *ibid.*

84. Cf. Brown, *ibid.*

85. Fitzmyer, *loc. cit.*

86. *Loc. cit.*

87. Cf. R. Horsley and J. Hanson, *Bandits, Prophets and Messiahs: Popular Messianic Movements in the Time of Jesus* (1985), p. 91. This says nothing about the *accuracy* of such listings—only that a record of priestly lineage would be considered important for priestly families, both for male and female members if Luke 1:5 reflects Palestinian priestly practice at the time.

88. cf. *SC Syn G*, pp. 106, 110.

89. Cf. e.g. *Birth*, pp. 90, 92.

90. This fact will be seen to be important later in the discussion of Jesus' debate with the Scribes concerning the Davidic lineage of the Messiah (Mark 12:35-37).

91. Cf. the extended discussions e.g. in Brown, *Birth*, pp. 547-556; Fitzmyer, *Luke 1*, pp. 392f., 389-405; Marshall, *op. cit.*, pp. 97-104.

92. Cf. e.g. the discussion in Brown, *Birth*, pp. 35-37.

93. *Op. cit.,* p. 107. Brown (*Birth*, pp. 418f.) and Fitzmyer (*Luke 1*, p. 408) prefer the term 'lodging,' and Fitzmyer, at least, understands Luke's meaning to be "a public caravansary or khan."

94. M. Hengel, "PHATNE" in *Theological Dictionary of the New Testament*, Vol. IX (1974), p. 50.

95. The reality of the divine and supernatural in these accounts cannot be proven or disproven at this late date. The personal claim of Paul, e.g., to have had many visions (2 Cor. 12:1-4) shows that for Jews of his day such experiences were for them a reality. In the case of the infancy narratives these may have been part of the traditions the writers received (they are common to both Matthew and Luke to some

degree—cf. Brown's common core, *Birth*, pp. 34f.) or are their own literary creations.

96. The "manger" (*phatnē*) would be located in a room for domestic animals either under the living quarters or next to the living quarters which surrounded a courtyard. Such a room could be used as an additional guest room when needed. Cf. e.g. J. Holladay "House, Israelite," *Anchor Bible Dictionary* (1992), Vol. 3, pp. 310-313 especially for floor plans; cf. also A. Bouquet, *Everyday Life in New Testament Times* (1955), pp. 28-31; H. Daniel-Rops, *Daily Life in Palestine at the Time of Christ* (1962), pp. 220f. Cf. especially Hengel, *op. cit.*, p. 52 for archeological evidence for the type of Palestinian homes and the multi-use of animal quarters at the time of Jesus and pp. 51f. for Rabbinic descriptions; also note 26, p. 52.

97. This uncertainty may also be reflected in Mark 6:3 where "contrary to usual custom, Jesus is called the son of Mary rather than the son of Joseph." F. Filson, *A New Testament History* (1964), p. 90, though he explains this as due to the probable death of Joseph by this time.

98. *Op. cit.*, p. 438.

99. As Marshall notes about the Temple visit at twelve: "In itself the story is a natural one, and does not include any supernatural features... It portrays a growth in religious understanding such as might be expected in Jesus in view of his later life... Both setting and contents are thoroughly Jewish." *Op. cit.*, p. 126. It may be noted the Greek of this story is translation Greek. *SC Syn G*, p. 106, no. 18.

100. *Ibid.*

101. *SC Syn G*, p. 106, no. 10.

102. Reference to Mary at the cross occurs only in John's Gospel; some possibly negative references to her occur in Mark 3:31-35 (par. Mt. 12:46ff.; Lk 8:19ff.) and John 2:4.

103. Cf. e.g. Fitzmyer, *Luke 1*, p. 450; Marshall, *op. cit.*, pp. 131f.;

Meier, *op. cit.*, p. 89.

104. Cf. J. A. T. Robinson, "The Baptism of John and the Qumran Community" in *Harvard Theological Review*, Vol. 50 (1957), pp. 175-191 *re* the usefulness of the Fourth Gospel particularly for a study of John the Baptist.

105. *SC Syn G*, p. 106 nos. 2, 3, 7, 8. Cf. also Marshall, *op. cit.*, p. 46: "However, the narratives betray a Semitic background to a degree unparalleled elsewhere in Lk-Acts. The whole atmosphere of the story is Palestinian. The language too is strongly Semitic..." Cf. also the detailed comments concerning the Semitic Greek sections of Luke in the Introduction *supra*, pp. 3f.

106. Crossan places the traditions about John's appearance and early ministry in his "first stratum" of evidence (i.e. 30-60 C.E.) Cf. *op. cit.*, pp. 427, 437 no. 51. They are by his listing triply attested (Gospel of Thomas 78; Q; Mark) and marked with a + sign, indicating in his judgment that they reflect authentic tradition. Brown, further, finds authentic John the Baptist material also in various places in John's Gospel. Cf. his *John 1, passim.* Cf. also the judgment of Robinson, *op. cit.*, p. 190.

107. The other persons mentioned in 3:1f. do not enable any closer dating than this notice concerning Tiberius. Cf. Marshall, *op. cit.*, p. 133. Fitzmyer notes correctly: "We have no idea where Luke might have come upon this dating" (*Luke 1*, p. 455). Luke's later reference (3:2) that John the Baptist is the son of Zechariah, however, may connect it to the early Semitic traditions of chapter 1, noted *supra*, pp. 8f.

108. Cf. *ibid.*, pp. 455f. Cf. also Marshall, *ibid.*

109. Fitzmyer indicates such a procedure "seems to be unlikely, but cannot be wholly excluded." *Ibid.*, p. 455.

110. Donfried (*op. cit.*, p. 1013) puts it a year earlier: "If on the basis of Vellaius Paterculus (2.121) this date is assigned to 11 C.E. or on the basis of Suetonius (*Tib.* 21) to 12 C.E., the Baptist's activity

would then be placed in the period 25-26 C.E. Cf. also Caird, *op. cit.*, p. 601.

111. Fitzmyer, *ibid.*; Marshall, *ibid.* Both indicate most scholars prefer this dating.

112. He prefers this dating. Cf. *ibid.* and the holders of this view cited there. Brown also prefers this dating. *John 1*, p. 116.

113. 20/19 is the 18th year of Herod's reign according to *Ant.* If the less probable 15th year of Herod's reign is taken to be the date he began the project (*Wars*), then the date would be 23/22 B.C.E. Cf. Donfried, *op. cit.*, p. 1014.

114. Cf. also Caird, *op. cit.*, p. 601; also R. A. Martin, "The Date of the Cleansing of the Temple in John 2:13-22" in *Indian Journal of Theology*, Vol. XV, 1966, pp. 53f. and esp. notes 13, 14, p. 54.

115. Cf. e.g. Haenchen, *John 1*, p. 184; Brown, *John 1*, pp. 115f.

116. Cf. Fitzmyer's discussion, *Luke 1*, p. 459. Flusser improbably locates John's activity at the northern end of the Sea of Galilee. *Jesus* (1969), pp. 30f.

117. Brown points out that this is a different place than the Bethany near Jerusalem and is "a site of which no trace remains." (*John 1*, p. 44). After noting various identifications he points out the notice should not be summarily dismissed since "Scholars have become more cautious now that some Johannine place names, once accounted to be purely symbolic (e.g. Bethesda 5:2), have been shown to be factual." *Ibid.*, p. 45. Cf. also K. Clark, "Bethany," *Interpreter's Dictionary of the Bible* (1962), Vol. 1, p. 388.

118. This Aenon is usually located near the Jordan in Judea because of the preceding verse (cf. M.Avi-Jonah, "Aenon," *Interpreter's Dictionary of the Bible*, [1962], Vol. 1, p. 52). Brown rejects this identification and prefers the Samaria location, since if an area near the Jodan were meant "John's mention of the availability of water seems superfluous." *John 1*, p. 151. About the Samaria site he writes: "Four

miles east-southeast of Shechem there is a town of Salim known from early times, eight miles northeast of Salim lies modern 'Ainun. In the general vicinity there are many springs, although modern 'Ainun has no water." *Ibid.*

119. *Op. cit.*, p. 30; cf. also Brown, *John 1,* p. 151; A. Koester, *History and Literature of Early Christianity* (1982), Vol. 2, p. 70: "The information that John was active as an eschatological prophet, not only in Judea, but also in other parts of Palestine, is historically reliable."

120. *John 1*, p. 45. Concerning the Fourth Gospel he notes: "Little of this appears in John; for the evangelist is not interested in John the Baptist as a baptizer or as a prophet but only in his being a herald of Jesus..." *Ibid.*

121. *Op. cit.*, p. 73.

122. *Ibid.*

123. Brown writes: "There are many links, geographical and ideological, that connect John the Baptist to these Essenes [of Qumran]; and without necessarily having been an Essene, John the Baptist may well have been influenced by contact with them." *John 1*, p. 49. Fitzmyer suggests "it is not unlikely that John, the son of Zechariah... spent some time among the Essenes in the desert of Judah until God's call came to him." *Op. cit.*, p. 453. Cf. also W. Brownlee, "John the Baptist in the Light of Ancient Scrolls" in *The Scrolls and the New Testament* ed. by K. Stendahl (1957), p. 35; Robinson, *op. cit.*, pp. 190f.

124. Cf. J. Murphy-O'Connor "Qumran, Khirbet," *Anchor Bible Dictionary* (1992), Vol. 5, pp. 590-594.

125. Vermes lists 13 coins from 132-103 B.C.E.; 153 coins from 103-37 B.C.E.; 10 coins from 37-4 B.C.E.; 16 coins from 4 B.C.E. to 6 C.E.; 263 coins from 6-69 C.E.; a few Roman coins 69-74 C.E.; a few coins 132-135 C.E. "Dead Sea Scrolls," *Interpreter's Dictionary of the Bible. Supplement* (1976), p. 210. He concluded: "The numismatic evidence therefore yields solid backing to the thesis that the Qumran settlement was founded in the second half of the

second century B.C.E. and remained occupied, possibly without interruption, until the war of 66-70 C.E., but more probably until 68 C.E." *Ibid.* Murphy-O'Connor indicates the buildings of Ib were occupied about 100 B.C.E. and concludes that "the beginning of Period Ia must be placed sometime in the second half of the 2nd century B.C.E." *Op. cit.*, p. 591. Cf. also J. Collins, "Essenes," *Anchor Bible Dictionary* (1992), Vol. 2, p. 625. He places the beginnings a bit earlier "in the early 2nd century B.C.E."

126. J. Collins, *loc. cit.*

127. Cf. e.g. Hengel (referring to fragments from cave IV): "At a time when the activity of the Zealots was becoming more intense throughout the whole country, then the Essenes seemed to have evolved certain ideas about the eschatological war against Rome, which were not so far removed from those of the Zealots." *Zealots* (1989), pp. 276f. This does not mean the community became a Zealot community, however. Cf. R. de Vaux, *Archeology and the Dead Sea Scrolls* (1973), pp. 117ff.

128. Murphy-O'Connor, *op. cit.*, p. 593.

129. *Ibid.*

130. *Ibid.*, p. 591.

131. Cf. *Ibid.* An earthquake in the area is dated in 31 B.C.E. by Josephus (*Wars*) *Ibid.* Since neighboring Khirbet Feshka (which was a farming/industrial support settlement for Qumran) was not destroyed, military action is unlikely to have caused the destruction and abandonment. *Ibid.* Cf. also Collins, *op. cit.*, p. 626.

132. Prior to Herod it is clear that "for the sectaries, the temple of Jerusalem singled out by Jewish law as the sole place of sacrificial worship, was a place of abomination; its precincts were considered polluted, its priests wicked and the liturgical calendar prevailing there unlawful." Vermes, *op. cit.*, p. 215. Cf. also Collins, *op. cit.*, p. 624.

133. Cf. R. Reisner, "Essene Gate," *Anchor Bible Dictionary* (1992),

Vol. 2, p. 619. He writes: "Essene Gate bears the name of an Essene settlement in the immediate vicinity. The archeological data support the assumption that this quarter was erected at the beginning of the reign of Herod the Great (39-34 B.C.E.), who, according to Josephus, had a friendly attitude toward the Essenes (*Ant.* 15.371-378). For the duration of his reign the monastic settlement at Qumran remained abandoned, a circumstance that would also support the possibility of an Essene settlement in the holy city."

134. Cf. Murphy-O'Connor, *op. cit.*, p. 593.

135. Cf. de Vaux, *op. cit.*, p. 122. There is some disagreement on when the Zealots first appeared. While most interpret Josephus as indicating a connection with the 6 C.E. revolt (cf. e.g. H. Merkel "Zealot" in *Interpreter's Dictionary of the Bible. Supplement* [1992], pp. 979-982), R. Horsley considers them to have become a movement during the 66-70 C.E. revolt. "Messianic Movements in Judaism" in *Anchor Bible Dictionary* (1992), Vol. 4, p. 793.

136. Since the traditions show Zachariah, his father, to have been a rural priest (1:5, 39) serving in the Temple under Aaronic priests appointed by Herod the Great, it is possible that he had Essene leanings and would not have favored the corrupt Hasmonean High Priests of the pre-Herod days.

137. M. de Jonge writes: "We should also be careful in employing the words 'eschatology' and 'eschatological'. The basic element in the expectations which are commonly called 'eschatological' is the conviction that God will complete and crown his dealings with the whole world by effecting a radical and lasting change, inaugurating a new era. God may use real human or angelical intermediaries in bringing about this change, but often agents of divine deliverance are not found at all." "Messiah" in *Anchor Bible Dictionary* (1993), Vol. 4, p. 778.

138. "Belief in a substantial, meaningful existence after death is a relatively late development in the history of Israelite religion. The usual view expressed in the biblical books is that, upon death, one's shade descends to Sheol, where one remains forever, cut off from God's

presence." G. Nickelsburg, "Resurrection (Early Judaism and Christianity," *Anchor Bible Dictionary* (1992), Vol. 5, p. 685; cf. also R. Martin-Achard, "Resurrection (OT)," *ibid.*, p. 683: "Between Hosea and Daniel the resurrection cropped up here and there, but chiefly to point toward the political renewal of the people of Israel (Ezekiel)... The existence of shades in Sheol, mentioned many times, noticeably in the Psalms, was the total opposite of life—a kind of 'nonlife'—out of which no positive element could arise."

139. Vermes writes: "Finally, whereas there is ample evidence that the [Qumran] sect imagined the post-messianic age in the form of a new Jerusalem, there is no definite indication of any central belief in bodily resurrection... Consequently, nothing sure is known at the present time of the community's attitude to the destiny after death of the saints of past ages." *Op. cit.*, p. 216. Cf. Collins, *op. cit.*, pp. 622, 624; also Nickelsburg, *op. cit.*, p. 687. Since the community is dominated by *priests* it is not surprising that little is said about resurrection; any intimations concerning a belief in life after death at Qumran may be the reflection of the variety of conservative Jews who over the years were attracted to the group.

140. Brown remarks concerning John the Baptist himself speaking this Old Testament passage in John 1:23: "Now, however, we know that it is perfectly plausible that John the Baptist did use the text of himself. The Qumran Essenes used precisely this text to explain why they chose to live in the desert: they were preparing the way for the Lord by studying and observing the Law (1 QS viii 13-16)." *John 1*, p. 50. Cf. also Fitzmyer, *Luke 1*, pp. 452ff.

141. *Luke 1*, p. 389. He notes that John's actually having lived among the Essenes for a while "cannot be proved or disproved;" but he appears to consider it probable. Cf. *ibid.*, pp. 389, 453ff.

142. Referring to 11 Q Melch Brooke notes: "The whole text is eschatological, concerning the 'latter days' (*aharit hayyamim*). For the Sons of Light, Melchizedek will proclaim release and make expiation; for Belial and those of his lot, Melchizedek will exact the vengeance of the judgments of God. In this dualistic struggle... Melchizedek will act as God's agent. All this will happen in the tenth and last possible

period in which in the seventh part of the tenth week the eternal judgment is executed by the angels... In addition, Melchizedek is accompanied by one who brings good news (*mbśr*), the anointed one (*hmšyh*), who may be the Teacher of Righteousness, or the eschatological prophet, or the Davidic Messiah."   G. Brooke "Melchizedek (11 Q Melch)," *Anchor Bible Dictionary* (1992), Vol. 4, p. 687. This fragment is dated paleographically to the "first half of the 1st century C.E. (van der Woude)" but the text itself was probably "composed about 120 B.C.E. (Milik, Puech)." *Ibid.*

143. Cf. e.g. Brown (*John 1*, p. 50) with ref. to 1 QS ix.11."..until the coming of a prophet and the messiahs of Aaron and Israel." Cf. also Vermes, *op. cit.*, p. 216.

144. Cf. the evidence for such claims after the 1st Christian century in Brown, *ibid.*, pp. 46f. Cf. also G. Friedrich "EUAGGELIZOMAI" in *Theological Dictionary of the New Testament*, Vol. 2 (1971), p. 719.

145. Cf. e.g. W. Flemington, "Baptism," *Interpreter's Dictionary of the Bible* (1962), Vol. 1, pp. 348f.

146. Fitzmyer, *Luke 1*, p. 460.

147. *Ibid.*, p. 459. He writes: "A number of Jewish and Christian groups emerged in this period that practiced some form of ritual washing. Though the forms differed and the connotations to them varied, the washings of the Essenes, of John and his disciples..., of Jesus and his disciples..., of the Ebionites and a host of later Gnostic groups are examples of this general movement." *Ibid.*, pp. 459f.

148. *Jeremias, op. cit.*, p. 43.

149. *Ibid.* Cf. also Fitzmyer, *Luke 1*, p. 454; Flusser, *op. cit.*, p. 25.

150. *Ibid.*, p. 44.

151. Whether this preparation meant they had already repented and were living repentant lives or intended to live repentant lives from then onwards, while frequently debated, is not able to be determined by the

sketchy data available. Cf. e.g. Jeremias, *op. cit.*, p. 43; Marshall, *op. cit.*, p. 137; Crossan, *op. cit.*, p. 23; Fitzmyer, *Luke 1*, pp. 459f.

152. Cf. e.g. J. Schneider, "ERCOMAI," *Theological Dictionary of the New Testament*, Vol. II (1971), p. 667; Friedrich, *op. cit.*, p. 716; Brown, *John 1*, p. 46; E. Schweizer, *The Good News according to Matthew* (1977), p. 51; Fitzmyer, *Luke 1*, pp. 666f.

153. Cf. Crossan, *op. cit.*, p. 235; Koester, *op. cit.*, p. 70.

154. Cf. e.g. E. Haenchen, *op. cit.*, Vol. 1, pp. 147f.: "This mighty figure could not have been Yahweh himself. One cannot compare man with God."

155. Cf. Brown, *John 1*, pp. 44, 47f.; Fitzmyer, *Luke 1*, pp. 472, 477. It is not clear, however, that Elijah was to judge and destroy evil doers, rather than only announce the coming of the One who would (cf. Mal. 3:1-5; 4:1-6).

156. Cf. Brown, *John 1*, p. 46; Schneider, *op. cit.*, pp. 660, 667; S. Mowinckel, *He That cometh (1959), passim*; Marshall, *op. cit.*, p. 132; Fitzmyer, *Luke 1*, pp. 466, 472f. Brown, however, writes: "There is not much evidence, however, that John [the Baptist] identified the one to come after him as the Messiah in the strict sense, i.e., anointed Davidic king. John iii 28 is the only specific reference to John the Baptist's preparing the way for the Messiah; it may be implied in Luke iii 15-16." *John 1*, p. 43. For the strictest meaning of the terms 'Messiah/Messianic' cf. also de Jonge, *op. cit.*, p. 778; Horsley, "Messianic," p. 791.

157. Cf. e.g. Brown, *John 1*, p. 57; Fitzmyer, *Luke 1*, p. 473.

158. Fitzmyer, *ibid.*, pp. 473-475.

159. Cf. Marshall, *op. cit.*, pp. 146f.

160. Cf. Flusser, *op. cit.*, pp. 28f.; Marshall, *op. cit.*, p. 147; Fitzmyer, *Luke 1*, pp. 473f. with specific ref. to 1 QS 4:20-21.

161. *Ibid.*, p. 454.

162. Cf. Marshall's survey, *op. cit..*, pp. 141f. Cf. also Fitzmyer, *Luke 1*, p. 464.

163. Sanders lists it among "the undoubted facts" about Jesus. *Op. cit.*, p. 11. Cf. also Koester, *op. cit.,* p. 73; Crossan, *op. cit.*, 232ff.: "One conclusion emerges from the texts in that first unit: Jesus' baptism by John is one of the surest things we know about them both." *Ibid.*, p. 234. Jeremias, *op. cit.*, p. 45; Haenchen, *John*, Vol. 1, p. 148.

164. Jeremias, *ibid.*; Crossan, *ibid.*, p. 232; Kümmel, *op. cit.*, p. 31.

165. Cf. Luke's passive construction in 3:21 and the interposing of the account of John's imprisonment out of place between the account of John's work and Jesus having been baptised (3:19f.). Matthew shows John to be very hesitant to baptize Jesus saying that he does not really need to be baptized. Cf. John 1:19ff.; also Haenchen, *John*, Vol. 1, p. 148.

166. Cf. *supra.*, pp. 19.

167. If Jesus' birth is dated ca. 7-5 B.C.E., his age would be ca. 32-34 by 26-28 C.E., the dates for John's appearance and baptizing. Caird notes that in Qumran one needed to be 30 years of age before being "eligible for positions of religious leadership (CD XVII. 5. 6.)." *Op. cit.*, p. 601.

168. All the gospels witness to John's popularity, as does Josephus who says that Herod arrested John "when others too joined the crowds about him, because they were aroused to the highest degree by his sermons (*Ant.* 18. 116-119)." Cf. Crossan, *op. cit.*, pp. 230f.

169. The notice in Matt. 3:14f. that Jesus appears to accept John's statement that he has no need to undergo this baptism, is, as indicated in n. 165, Matthew's way of countering excessive Baptist veneration in the church of his day (ca. 85C.E.). Cf. Schweizer, *Matthew*, p. 53.

170. Schweizer writes: "Jesus went to John to be baptized, thereby

affirming John's message." *Jesus*, p. 22. Cf. J. O'Neill, *Messiah* (1980), p. 12. Similarly B. Meyer, *The Aims of Jesus* (1979), pp. 127f. So also Crossan, *op. cit.*, p. 237.

171. Gospel of Thomas 46: "Jesus said: From Adam to John the Baptist there is none born of woman who is greater than John the Baptist." Cf. K. Aland, *Synopsis Quattuor Evangeliorum* (1969), p. 523. Crossan considers the Q statement to "derive from the historical Jesus." *Op. cit.*, p. 237. Cf. also the Q statement in Lk. 16:16; Matt. 11:12f. and Jeremias' comments, *op. cit.*, p. 46ff.; also O' Neill, *op. cit.*, pp. 9ff.

172. Cf. e.g. Fitzmyer, *Luke 1*, pp. 1272f.: "As others have often noted... There is no reason to contest the authenticity of this account of Jesus' altercation with the Jerusalem authorities or the substance of the dialogue. Its roots and details are to be traced to stage I of the gospel tradition." Cf. also Jeremias, *op. cit.*, pp. 55f.

173. *Jesus*, p. 22; cf. also Kümmel, *op. cit.*, p. 32.

174. He writes: "But we know the principal context of Jesus' work: Jewish eschatology... the line from John the Baptist to Paul and the other early apostles is the line of Jewish eschatology, and it would be misleading to move the centre of our investigation off that line." *Op. cit.*, p. 8.

175. The Johannine presentation, however, has John publicly declare Jesus' special role sometime *after* he became aware of it at the time of the Spirit's descent on Jesus in his baptism. Whether this detail is traditional or a Johannine construction cannot be determined.

176. Cf. e.g. Brown, *John 1*, p. 58; cf. also pp. xliiff.; Haenchen, *op. cit.*, p. 155; R. Fortna, *op. cit.*, p. 119.

177. John's Gospel also reflects this same hesitancy, but in a different way—God had to tell John (1:33f.); and later (5:33f.) Jesus while acknowledging that John did testify to him, states he has no *need* for that or any other human witness. These passages confirm that the writer of the Fourth Gospel in these instances is dealing with a tradition

which he finds a bit embarrassing.

178. O'Neill (*op. cit.*, p. 8) and Brown (*John 1*, pp. 58ff.) e.g. both consider John to have done so.

179. In the Fourth Gospel, the Baptist says that he did not know Jesus until the Spirit's descent in the act of baptizing Jesus. This need not conflict with Jesus and John being related. It is most probable that what John the Baptist means is that he had no idea that his cousin Jesus was the Coming One. Cf. also Brown, *ibid.*, p. 65, though there he prefers the explanation that they may actually have been unacquainted before this time due to John's growing up "as a solitary in the Desert of Judea, apart from family contacts."

180. Cf. Martin, *SC Syn G*, p. 107, no. 28. Cf. also the special remarks *re* Luke-Acts data in *Syn Ev*, p. 99; *SC Syn G*, p. 69 and note 1.

181. This is an interesting passage since it suggests that an actual sound may be variously interpreted by listeners as an actual, meaningful message (Jesus) an angel (and unintelligible) or thunder (by bystanders). Rabbinic traditions frequently speak of revelations by means of Bat Qol (a heavenly voice). Cf. e.g. L. Blau, "Bat Kol," *Jewish Encyclopedia*, Vol. II (1902), p. 588.

182. Cf. the analysis in Martin, *SC Syn G*, pp. 68-71; cf. also Fitzmyer's discussion (*Luke*, pp. 790-801) where he concludes: "Given the diversity of the way in which the incident is reported, no real historical judgment can be made about it; to write it all off as mythical is likewise to go beyond the evidence. Just what sort of an incident in the ministry of Jesus—to which it is clearly related—it was is impossible to say." *Ibid.*, p. 796. Cf. also Marshall, *op. cit.*, p. 380f.

183. *Op. cit.*, pp. 49f. Cf. Brown (*John 1*, pp. 65f.) for the independence of the Johannine tradition concerning Jesus' baptism.

184. *Ibid.*, p. 51.

185. So also the striking physical aspect of the Spirit's descent

variously represented in the Gospels.

186. The Johannine tradition does not exclude this possibility, since the first mention of John's contact with Jesus (1:29) shows Jesus had been baptized sometime earlier (1:31-34).

187. Cf. e.g. Fitzmyer, *Luke 1*, p. 476.

188. Meyer correctly highlights this matter: "The Synoptic gospels date the start of Jesus' public career from the arrest of John... leaving unexplained why Jesus had remained in Judea until John's arrest... and why the arrest should have had particular and decisive significance for him." *Op. cit.*, p. 122.

189. This is clearly evident in the fact that John the Baptist, Jesus and the writer all sound the same—very Johannine—for example, in John 3:3-21; 3:27-36. Brown admits this when he writes: "Nevertheless it is still true that the fourth evangelist is the theologian par excellence. In particular, the formation of the sayings of Jesus into the Johannine discourses represented a profound theological synthesis." *John 1*, p. xlix. He remarks the great difference between the way Jesus speaks in the Synoptics and John. *Ibid*, p. xliii.

190. Haenchen: "The Evangelist did not freely create his narrative material, but more or less freely formed it while making use of tradition." *Op cit.*, p. 90. Barrett: "His narratives are for the most part simple, and the details remain unallegorized. This means that the chronicler can sometimes (though less frequently than is often thought) pick out from John simple and sound historical material." *Op. cit.*, p. 141.

191. Cf. Brown, *ibid.*, pp. xlixf. Barrett: "Since the material is disposed in accordance with a theological and literary scheme, it is idle to seek in John a *chronology* [italics added] of the ministry of Jesus. This is not to deny the existence of valuable historical material in John..." *Op. cit.*, p. 15.

192. Cf. e.g. Donfried, *op. cit.*, p. 1014 and Caird, *op. cit.*, p. 602, both of whom posit more than one, but not more than two years.

Brown legitimately notes "there is no real reason why one cannot postulate a four-or five year ministry." *John 1*, p. 1. All of this corresponds well with the postulated dating of Jesus' baptism between 26-28 C.E. and his death in 30 C.E.; cf. *supra*, p. 19.

193. *Op. cit.*, p. 74.

194. *Op. cit.*, p. 440.

195. Jeremias, *op. cit.*, p. 69. E. Schweizer writes: "The tradition of the community was probably limited originally to the bare fact of Jesus' temptation (cf. Heb. 2:18; 4:15; also 11:17). *Matthew*, p. 58. V. Taylor while granting the Markan account could be an abbreviated form of Q, prefers "as seems more probable, he would have been glad to use [Q], but was familiar only with the fact of the temptation by Satan as part of the catechetical tradition of the church, a possibility favoured by the rythmical form of the narrative." *The Gospel according to St. Mark* (1981), p. 163. Cf. also W. Lane, *The Gospel according to Mark* (1974), p. 59. H. Anderson, *The Gospel of Mark*, p. 80.

196. *Op. cit.*, p. 69; cf. also note 1.

197. Cf. no. 116, *op. cit.*, p. 440. Following Kloppenborg, he finds "three successive layers in its [Q's] development: a sapiential layer (1Q), an apocalyptic layer (2Q), and an introductory layer (3Q)..." *Ibid.*, p. 429.

198. J. Kloppenborg, *The Formation of Q* (1987), p. 59.

199. *Ibid.*, p. 64.

200. Cf. his survey *ibid.*, pp. 59-64.

201. Coordinating particles, subject-verb word order, separation of the article, position of attributive adjectives and genitive pronouns, hyperbata. *Ibid.*

202. *Ibid.*

203. This 58% is only the *certainly* translated Greek in Q. In the initial study it was found that the methodology of syntax criticism *left undetected up to 54% (Hebrew), 58% (Aramaic)* of smaller sections (4-15 lines) in documents known to be translated from Hebrew/Aramaic. Cf. *Syn Ev*, p. 52.

204. For a listing of all the units of Q material as analyzed by the method of "syntax criticism" see my *Syntax Criticism of the Synoptic Gospels*, (pp. 91-95) which was published in 1987 and thus was not available for Kloppenborg's study which came out in the same year.

205. Cf. *SC Syn G*, p. 91, no. 2.

206. So Kloppenborg, *op. cit.*, p. 248 and Crossan, *op. cit.*, p. 440.

207. Kloppenborg correctly notes that the stage in which material was taken up into the Q document does *"not* imply anything about the ultimate tradition-historical provenance of any of the sayings. It is indeed possible, indeed *probable* [italics added], that some of the material from the secondary compositional phase are dominical or at least very old..." *Ibid.*, p. 244. While these cautions refer to material in Kloppenborg's stage 2 of Q, they apply equally well to any material taken up into the final compilation of the Q source.

208. *Op. cit.*, p. 75.

209. E.g. Fitzmyer, *Luke 1*, p. 510. Crossan in explaining his use of the symbol ± for the temptation traditions writes: "It means that the action or happening did not occur as an event at one moment in time or place (hence -) but that it represents a dramatic historization of something that took place over a much longer period (hence +)." *Op. cit.*, p. 434. Cf. also Schweizer, *Matthew*, p. 65.

210. *Op. cit.*, p. 73.

211. He writes: "They [the temptation accounts] symbolize the seduction in the hostility, opposition and rejection which confronted him constantly *throughout his ministry* [italics added]. These are the elements that should be regarded as the 'real basis in the life of Jesus.'"

Loc. cit. Cf. also Marshall, *op. cit.*, p. 477; Crossan, *loc. cit.*

212. Luke's conclusion to Q (4:13) also clearly indicates that Satan was not 'vanquished' in an initial encounter.

213. Cf. e.g. the Qumran writing "The War of the Sons of Light against the Sons of Darkness" (dated ca. 50 B.C.E.).

214. It is unclear if Fitzmyer would agree or disagree with such a statement, for he writes: "The scenes depict temptations of Jesus coming from external sources; they do not suggest that they proceed from an inner conflict." (*op. cit.*, p. 510); but a bit later he writes "To understand the temptations or the testings of Jesus in this way ["parabolic fashion"] means they did not take place as a real, external happening in which the devil in some visible form encountered Jesus..." *Ibid.* Marshall would, however, agree when he speaks of this event as "an inner experience" and he correctly notes: "It is also probable that at the outset of his work he had to face up to the nature of his vocation... Behind the story lies the experience of Jesus, although the formulation of it will owe something to the early church." *Op. cit.*, p. 168.

215. Cf. chapter 2 *supra*.

216. Cf. the Psalms of Solomon (dated ca 50 B.C.E.), nos. 17, 18 where Davidic military leadership is still referred to.

217. So Merkel, *op. cit*, p. 980; also Hengel, *Zealots*, p. 144; Horsely, however sees the origin of the Zealots *as a group* in connection with the revolt of 66-70 C.E., though its beginnings in some sense are earlier. Horsley, "Messianic," p. 793.

218. The entire period 1-66 C.E. sees an increasing number of "Messianic" movements in Israel directed in some sense against Roman rule and making various appeals to the people for their support. Cf. Horsley, *ibid.*, cf. also his "Popular Messianic Movements," *Catholic Biblical Quarterly*, Vol. 46 (1984), pp. 471-495 and his detailed study with J. Hanson, *Bandits, Prophets and Messiahs* (1985). This kind of activity was centered primarily in Jerusalem. S. Freyne, *Galilee: From*

Alexander the Great to Hadrian (1980). Hengel writes that the expectation of a political Messiah "seems to have been concentrated above all on the ruler from the house of David who could also appear as leader in the eschatological war." *Zealots*, p. 29.

219. "Messianic Movements," p. 794.

220. Cf. e.g. Jeremias, *op. cit.*, p. 71 (cf. also pp. 68-75); Taylor, *op. cit.*, p. 380.

221. Cf. e.g. Anderson, *op. cit.*, p. 217.

222. If the description of John's preaching in Lk. 3:10-14 is authentic, John clearly had no interest in the overthrow of Rome and its administrative system.

223. The reference to the Baptist in the past tense in John 5:33-35 would, then, be an indication of the death of John.

224. Sanders notes that one of the things "most securely known about Jesus... Jesus began his public work, as far as we have any information at all about it, in close connection with John the Baptist, probably as a disciple..." Op. cit., p. 91 (cf. also note 1, pp. 370f.). Similarly Koester, *op. cit.*, p. 73; Crossan, *op. cit.*, p. 238); Jeremias (*op. cit.*, p. 46): "...we cannot by any means view the connection between Jesus and John the Baptist as only a fleeting one. It is easy to understand why the synoptic gospels compress the encounter of the two men into the moment of Jesus' baptism. The tradition avoided, as far as possible, anything that might look like an equation of Jesus with the Baptist or even of a subordination of Jesus to him. Any reports of this kind were passed over or toned down."

225. Jeremias considers this detail from the Fourth Gospel to have "considerable intrinsic probability, especially as something similar is presupposed by Acts in the account of the restoration of the group of twelve (1:21f.)." *Ibid.*, p. 47.

226. Cf. e.g. Brown, *John 1*, pp. 77f.; Meyer, *op. cit.*, p. 122 and note 23, p. 283.

227. *John 1*, p. 155; cf. also p. 164. Cf. also Meyer, *op. cit.*, p. 283 who notes other details in the accounts that would hardly have been invented and support the view that the Gospel writer here is using an earlier tradition. Cf. also Jeremias, *op. cit.*, p. 46; R. Bultmann, *The Gospel of John* (1971), pp. 168f.; Barrett, *op. cit.*, pp. 219, 221, 230. Jeremias notes that "it is easier to understand the quite remarkable fact that the primitive community began to baptize after Easter if Jesus himself had already been active in administering baptism." *Ibid.*

228. Both Bultmann (*op. cit.*, p. 113) and Barrett (*op. cit.*, p. 189) consider this possible but both see its probable origin in non-Christian (Bultmann "heathen," *ibid.*, p. 118) origin. Brown considers some such event to have probably happened. *John 1*, pp. 101-103.

229. Cf. Brown, *ibid.*, pp. cxxxviif.

230. If taken in a non-Johannine sense (of any activity which has symbolic significance) sign here could refer to the cleansing of the Temple, which as will be seen below may well have occurred in this period, rather than where Mark and the other Synoptics locate it. Brown notes in this connection that the writer in 4:54 "seems to ignore these signs when it counts the healing of the royal official's son as the second sign Jesus had done." *Ibid.*, p. 126.

231. For those who hold this view cf. the surveys in Martin, "The Date of the Cleansing of the Temple," *op. cit.*, p. 52, note 1; Taylor, *op. cit.*, p. 461; also Haenchen's survey of studies, *John 1*, pp. 187ff. Cf. also Brown, *John 1*, p. 118; G. Beasley-Murray, *John in Word Biblical Commentary* (1987), Vol. 36, pp. 38f.

232. Cf. surveys in Taylor, *ibid.*, pp. 461f.; Haenchen, *ibid.*; and Fitzmyer, *Luke 2*, p. 1264.

233. Cf. e.g. Taylor, *op. cit.*, pp. 90-105 and pp. 147f.

234. *Op. cit.*, p. 1265. Cf. Taylor (*op. cit.*, pp. 461f.) for other details *versus* the Markan placement and supporting the Johannine location. The usual objection to John's is that he has a theological bias for locating it here. However, as H. Anderson notes, theological and

literary motivations are just as clear in the Synoptic presentations as well (*op. cit.*, p. 264). The argument that such action could only have led immediately to the arrest of Jesus and thus more suited to the Synoptic placement (e.g. Brown, *John 1*, p. 117), as will be seen below, may be an over-valuing of the amount of disturbance Jesus' activity would have caused. Cf. C. Mann, *Matthew* in *Anchor Bible* (1971), pp. 254f.; *Mark*, pp. 445f.

235. Cf. the discussion *supra*, p. 25. V. Eppstein proposes the Temple "cleansing" could only have happened in 30 C.E. when according to Rabbinical sources Caiaphas allowed sales in the court of Gentiles for the first time. "The Historicity of the Gospel Account of the Cleansing of the Temple" in *Zeitschrift für die Neutestamentliche Wissenschaft*, Vol. 55 (1964), pp. 42-58; but cf. Haenchen's critique of that view. *John 1*, p. 183.

236. *Op. cit.*, pp. 85f.

237. *Ibid.*, p. 86, note 1.

238. Dodd writes: "To sum up: there are sound reasons for the conclusion that in his account of the cleansing of the Temple John followed an independent strain of tradition, which probably contained both the narrative and a brief controversial dialogue provoked by it, the latter probably ending with the saying, 'Destroy this temple...' In all probability Mark had a corresponding tradition of action and dialogue, but he has separated them in the course of composition, and his variant form of the saying is incorporated in his Passion narrative." C. H. Dodd, *Historical Tradition in the Fourth Gospel* (1963), pp. 161f.; cf. the detailed discussion pp. 89, 91 and 160.

239. Cf. *op. cit.*, p. 86 and *Ergängzungsheft*, p. 18.

240. *Ibid.*

241. So e.g. Brown, *John 1*, p. 120; Fitzmyer, *Luke 2*, p. 1264; Bultmann, *op. cit.*, p. 122; Dodd, *op. cit.*, pp. 160ff. Barrett, however, disagrees (*op. cit.*, p. 195); cf. his discussion of the entire question of the relation of John to Mark, *ibid.*, pp. 15ff.

242. *Ibid.*, note 1. In fact John's account (2:13-22) is translation Greek as syntax criticism demonstrates. Cf. *SC Joh*, p. 9. The form of the story without vv. 18-22 is like Matthew and Mark, borderline translation Greek (cf. *SC Joh*, p. 48, no. 4). Luke has radically abridged the Markan account.

243. *Op. cit.*, p. 359; cf. also Eppstein, *op. cit.*, p. 44. Haenchen is one of a small minority rejecting its historicity. *John 1*, p. 190.

244. Mark 1:14 shows that at the very beginning of his ministry this was the message of Jesus' preaching also. It is significant that Luke has the disciples concerned about this kind of a message even in the days immediately after the resurrection: "Will you at this time restore the kingdom to Israel" (Acts 1:6)? certainly implying this has been at least a part of Jesus' preaching.

245. *Op. cit.*, p. 264.

246. *Ibid.* Mann (*Mark*, p. 447) characterizes it as "a brief attack on a small scale, momentarily disrupting business...." Again, the incident "probably did not attract much attention apart from its immediate environment... and Jesus' action, apart from those close to him, may have appeared to be no more than a passing incident." *Ibid.*, *Matthew*, pp. 254f.

247. Cf. e.g. Crossan, *op. cit.*, p. 357; Mann, *Mark*, p. 446; Sanders, *op. cit.*, p. 75.

248. Sanders (*op. cit.*, p. 89) indicates that both the cleansing and destruction of the Temple "point towards 'eschaton,' not purity." It is difficult to see, however, that in relation to the eschaton purity would not also have been an issue.

249. *Op. cit.*, pp. 86f.

250. Cf. J. H. Charlesworth, "Review" of E. Sanders, *Jesus and Judaism* in *Journal of the American Academy of Religion*, Vol. 55 (1987), p. 624.

251. Accepting the reading of the LXX for the second cleansing (v. 20). The MT is probably corrupt here. Cf. G. A. Cooke, *The Book of Ezekiel* in the *International Critical Commentary* (1951), pp. 502, 507. Cf. also R. G. Finch, *The Synagogue Lectionary and the New Testament* (1939), p. 68.

252. Cf. Finch, *ibid.*, pp. 21 and 33. That these lessons were in use even before the time of Jesus is shown by Finch, *ibid.*, pp. 2-9, especially p. 6 and by A. Guilding, *The Fourth Gospel and Jewish Worship* (1960), chs. 2 and 3.

253. This obduracy is clear from John's preaching as recorded in Q (Lk. 3:7; Matt. 3:7), Mark's account of Jesus' castigating the priests in the Temple because they rejected John's baptism and thereby his message (Mk. 11:27ff.), and from Jesus' apparent subsequent avoidance of Judea suggested both by the Synoptics and by the antagonism evident in the Fourth Gospel from chapter 5 onwards. Haenchen feels the Pharisees were also upset with Jesus' success in Judea "which exceeds that of John who is already under suspicion. They threaten persecution and for this reason Jesus has to quit Judea and return to Galilee." *John I*, pp. 217f. Cf. also Brown, *John 1*, p. 165; Bultmann, *op. cit.*, p. 176.

254. Meyer considers Jesus to have understood John's imprisonment "as a signal from God." *Op. cit.*, p. 283; cf. also Anderson, *op. cit.*, p. 83; Lane, *op. cit.*, p. 63.

255. It may be that Jesus and John disagreed on the importance of announcing the Kingdom in Galilee—John feeling as many Jews did that it was largely Gentile country; particularly after the destruction of the Northern Kingdom in 722 B.C.E. and the continued Gentile dominance there until its reconquest by the Maccabeans. Cf. Is. 9:1 (MT 8:23) "Galilee of the Gentiles" and John 1:46: "Can anything good come from Nazareth?"

256. Josephus and the Gospels disagree on various details of John's arrest, imprisonment and death. Cf. e.g. the discussions in Taylor, *op. cit.*, pp. 310f; Lane, *op. cit.*, 215ff.; Anderson, *op. cit.*, p. 166. Mann, *Mark*, pp. 295f.; Guelick, *Mark*, pp. 326ff. The difference with respect

to the cause of imprisonment and death (Josephus: fear of political unrest; Gospels: Herodias' anger) are not irreconcilable, as Mann notes: "Each account is compatible with the other and each complements the other." *Ibid.*, p. 296; cf. also Crossan, *op. cit.*, p. 232; Anderson, *ibid.*, Taylor, *ibid.*, p. 311; Fitzmyer, *Luke 1*, p. 451.

257.   The correct translation of the perfect tense of *eggidzo* (approach, come near) has been disputed.   Literally it would be translated "has come near" or "is near." The translation "is present" or "has arrived.," identifying the Kingdom with Jesus himself is improbable. Cf. the discussion in Taylor, *op. cit.*, pp. 166f. where he surveys Greek usage and concludes: "While, then, the translation 'has come' may be possible, it seems more likely that [the perfect] should be rendered 'is at hand' or 'has drawn near'..." Cf. also Anderson, who indicates this is the now generally accepted meaning" and preferable to the view of C.H. Dodd... leading advocate of 'realized eschatology'." *Op. cit.*, p. 86. Cf. also O. Evans "Kingdom of God," *Interpreter's Dictionary of the Bible*, Vol. 3 (1962), p. 20.

258.   So, for example, Koester, *op. cit.*, p. 73; Jeremias, *op. cit.*, pp. 47-49. Haenchen considers the change to have occurred earlier, already in connection with the baptism of Jesus. *John 1*, pp. 148f. Crossan puts it later in connection with the death of John. *Op. cit.*, pp. 237.

259.   Cf. e.g. the recent survey by D. Duling, "Kingdom of God, Kingdom of Heaven" in *Anchor Bible Dictionary*, Vol. 4, (1992), pp. 62ff.

260.   The danger is to *a priori* decide what Jesus could or could not have thought about the Kingdom and then to use that *a priori* assumption to discount divergent statements of Jesus on the basis of that *a priori* assumption alone. Cf. e.g. Funk, *op. cit.*, p. 58: "The Fellows of the Seminar are convinced that Jesus used the language and conceptuality of God's rule or domain (kingdom). At the same time, they generally doubt that Jesus expected the end of the world in his lifetime or soon thereafter. The conclusion they evidently draw is that, for Jesus, the rule of God was not the beginning of the new age within history or the end of history following a cosmic catastrophe. Nor did Jesus speak of God's rule in the nationalistic sense as a revival of

David's kingdom. Rather, Jesus must have spoken of God's rule as close or already present but hidden, and thus in a way that frustrates ordinary expectations."

261. Development is more probable than that Jesus "held both ideas in his mind [at the same time], sometimes emphasizing the one and at times the other" as Evans suggests. *Op. cit.*, p. 23.

262. The cautions of O'Neill [*Messiah* (1980), p. 52] and Sanders (*op. cit.*, p. 160) are well taken; yet, at the same time, the indications that are in the traditions should not be disregarded.

263. Further changes in Jesus' expectations concerning the arrival of the Kingdom are evident in later stages of his ministry as well—cf. chapter 5 *infra*.

264. Jewish speculation concerning the nearness of the end was frequently connected with apparent increases in the antagonism against God's faithful people. Cf. for example *Testament of Moses* 9:7ff. and the discussion by J. Priest in the "Introduction" to it in J. Charlesworth, *The Old Testament Pseudepigrapha*, Vol. 1 (1983), p. 923.

265. Cf. the discussion *supra* pp. 21ff.

266. De Jonge insists that the term Messiah should be used "only where the sources use the corresponding word in their own language" and that "'messianic expectation' should denote the expectation of a redeemer who is actually called 'Messiah.'" *Op. cit.*, p. 778. The term 'Messianic age' is used in this study, however, in a more general sense to refer to the expected future glorious period of life on earth, whether it is thought to be innaugurated by God directly or through a human agent. The term 'Kingdom of God', on the other hand, is used to indicate God's rule either on earth or in the future consummation of all things. Horsley ("Messianic Movements," p. 791) also indicates that it is useful to retain a *broader* use of these terms.

267. Dated ca 105-104 B.C.E. Cf. e.g. E. Isaac in Charlesworth, *Pseudepigrapha*, p. 1.

268. *Ibid.*, p. 73.

269. *Ibid.* The length of this Messianic rule on earth is variously indicated to be 400, 600 or 1000 years in Jewish traditions in the 1st century C.E.

270. As can be seen from passages in the Gospel traditions which show both Jesus and his disciples as speaking of such a rule on earth (e.g. Mark 10:29f., 36-40).

271. Qumran clearly shared 1 Enoch's expectation of violently participating in the defeat of evil in the last days—cf. The War Scroll ("The War of the Sons of Light against the Sons of Darkness"). Cf., for example, B. Metzger, "in Charlesworth, *Pseudepigrapha*, p. 521; Evans, *op. cit.*, p. 19; R. H. Charles, *Eschatology* (1970), *passim.* Raymond Martin, *Studies in the Life and Ministry of the Early Paul and Related Issues* (1993), pp. 115f. and the evidence cited there.

272. Except for the Temple cleansing which, as indicated *supra* pp. 36ff., probably belongs to the earlier Judean period when Jesus was a disciple of John the Baptist. The precise translation and meaning of the Q/Thomas saying concerning peace or sword (Lk. 12:51; Mt. 10:34; Thomas no. 10) is disputed, but appears to be associated more with the latest stage of Jesus' ministry. Cf. also Charlesworth, "Review," *op. cit.*, p. 623.

273. This may have been reflected already in the early tradition (so Bultmann, *op. cit.*, p. 169) in John 3:25 which appears to be a dispute "between some disciples of John and a Jew baptized by Jesus." Haenchen, *John 1* p. 210. Haenchen indicates it is probably over cleansing laws rather than baptism. *Ibid.* So also Barrett, *op. cit.*, p. 221; Brown, *John 1*, p. 151f.

274. *Op. cit.*, p. 182. Cf. also Freyne, *op. cit.*, pp. 306ff.

275. Cf. Crossan, *op. cit.*, p. 260; cf. also Meyer, *op. cit.*, p. 124 and note 37.

276. There can be little doubt that Jesus performed acts which Jews

of that day considered miraculous during his Galilean ministry. While it is correct, as Jeremias shows, that "when subjected to a critical literary and linguistic analysis, the content of the miracle stories diminishes quite considerably," he nevertheless concludes: "But even when critical methods have been applied with the utmost strictness and the material has been reduced accordingly, a *nucleus of tradition* still stands out which is firmly associated with the events of the ministry of Jesus" (*op. cit.*, p. 91), which is "a demonstrably historical nucleus" (*ibid.*, p. 92; cf. the entire discussion pp. 86-96).

277. Sanders considers this understanding on the part of Jesus to be "possible, but not provable." *Op. cit.*, p. 158. Funk (*op. cit.,* p. 85) prints the verses from Mark in pink, which means, on average, they "agree" that they "probably go back to the historical Jesus." *Ibid.*, p. xxi; also p. 54, no. 7.

278. So also Kümmel, *op. cit.*, p. 62.

279. W. Arndt and F.Gingrich, *A Greek-English Lexicon of the New Testament* (1957), p. 864.

280. *Op. cit.*, p. 434. Cf. no. 150, p. 442; also no. 121, p. 441. The entire passage concerning Beelzebul is translation Greek in both its Q form and in the Markan form (*SC Syn G,* no. 17, p. 42).

281. For the debate it has raised cf. the discussions in Fitzmyer, *Luke 2*, p. 922 and Marshall, *op. cit.*, p. 476.

282. For evidence of such exorcisms in Palestine at this time cf. e.g. Fitzmyer, *Luke 2*, pp. 921f.; also Marshall, *op. cit.*, p. 474. Sanders points to the fact of this accusation to establish the reality of Jesus' exorcist activity. *Op.cit.*, p. 272.

283. Thus, to impugn Jesus' exorcisms is *blasphemy* against the Holy Spirit, ascribing what the Spirit does to Satan's activity (Mk. 3:28-30 and parallels).

284. Cf. e.g. the citations of various occasions when Jesus does this in Jeremias, *op. cit.*, pp. 72ff. and Fitzmyer, *loc. cit.*

285. *Pace* Jeremias (*op. cit.*, p. 73). Cf. Taylor, *op. cit.*, pp. 241f.

286. Jeremias appears to consider it to refer to the initial wilderness testing experience of Jesus (*ibid.*, pp. 73f.). It more probably, as in the Lukan context, refers to a victory brought about in connection with the disciples' mission of proclamation from which they have just returned (cf. the reference to casting out demons, etc. Lk. 10:17; Mk. 6:13). Marshall favors this view. *Op. cit.*, pp. 428f. Fitzmyer considers it "a symbolic way of summing up the effects of the disciples' mission," rather than an actual vision. *Luke 2*, p. 860.

287. Cf. Jeremias, *op. cit.*, pp. 80-82. Marshall observes "Jesus may be claiming that the kingly rule of God is evident wherever the power of God is demonstrated." *Op. cit.*, pp. 474f.

288. Fitzmyer, citing Kümmel, correctly notes this story "contradicts the tendency of the early Church" which considers John to be a God-appointed witness to Jesus' nature and role and concludes: "So most probably the story in its essentials represents an old reliable tradition." *Luke 1*, pp. 663f. Cf. also Marshall, *op. cit.*, p. 238.

289. That Jesus performed healing miracles as well as excorcisms is strongly attested in the traditions: cf. the healing of the centurion's/nobleman's servant/son in Q (Lk. 7:1-10; Mt. 8:5-13) and John's Gospel (John 4:46-54)—both John and Matthew's form of Q are translation Greek (cf. *SC Joh*, p. 9 and no. 10 in *SC Syn G*, p. 91); cf. also the following Markan miracle stories all of which are translation Greek in one or more of the Synoptics: the cleansing of the leper—Lk. 5:12-15 (no. 9, *SC Syn G*, p. 42); the healing of the paralytic—-Mk. 2:1-12 (both the Markan and Lukan forms, *ibid.*, no. 10, p. 41); the curing of the woman's hemorrhage and the raising of Jairus' daughter—Mk. 5:21-43 (the Markan pericope and part of Matthew's, nos. 31-33, *ibid.*, p. 43). Crossan lists a number of them (110, 119, 127) in his first stratum with a + (*op. cit.*, p. 461). Miraculous healing is often associated with Jesus' excorcisms. This is due to the common Jewish view that sickness was generally caused by demons and/or a person's sin. Thus both exorcisms and miracles manifest God's activity through the Spirit, as Jesus claims here.

290. Fitzmyer, *ibid.*; Marshall, *ibid.* There is no indication in the traditions whether John before his death ever changed his expectations of Jesus and of God's coming reign. Cf. e.g. Kümmel, *op. cit.*, p. 31.

291. This is multiply attested in Crossan's opinion and designated with a +, indicating it goes back to the historical Jesus (no. 22, p. 436). By the 17 criteria of syntax criticism it is translation Greek, one of the most Semitic sections in Luke's Gospel (*SC Syn G*, p. 107, no. 20). Fitzmyer notes that Bultmann considered this to go back to a (probably) Aramaic tradition (*Luke 1*, p. 526) and thus Luke has reworked various earlier sources (including Mark). *Ibid.*, p. 527. For other views cf. his survey, *ibid.*; also the survey of Marshall, *op. cit.*, pp. 178-181.

292. In the Gospel of Thomas form of the saying (no. 113) the disciples ask the question. It is considered an authentic saying of Jesus e.g. by Crossan (cf. no. 8, p. 435; also p. 283); Fitzmyer, *Luke 2*, p. 1157. Cf. also the discussion in Marshall, *ibid.*, pp. 652ff.

293. For a survey of the various interpretations offered for this phrase cf. Fitzmyer, *Luke 2*, pp. 1161f.; Marshall, *op. cit.*, pp. 655f. Whether *entos* is taken as "in" or "among" does not affect the point under consideration here—it is already in some sense present i.e., has arrived.

294. Crossan suggests that the ending of John's ministry by his death evoked a crisis in Jesus' thinking, so that from the death of John onwards Jesus no longer thought of a future apocalyptic Kingdom, but rather a "sapiential Kingdom" here and now. He takes them as mutually exclusive in relation to Jesus' own understanding (*op. cit.*, p. 292), though he indicates they need not be (*ibid.*, p. 291). As will be shown below, the delay of the apocalyptic consummation of the Kingdom provides Jesus with the stimulus for and practice of teaching in detail about the nature of the Kingdom (i.e. the rule of God) in the present Age.

295. Cf. the earlier discussion *supra* pp. 42f. Concerning Mk. 9:1 Funk (*op. cit.*, p. 143) indicates the group was sharply divided with "a substantial black vote [cannot go back to Jesus] which was offset by a substantial pink vote [probably goes back to Jesus]... the resulting

weighted average was of course gray [probably does not go back to the historical Jesus]."

296. Cf. e.g. Mt. 12:32; Lk. 20:34f.; 16:8 also. Paul and the early Christians had to make a similar adjustment because they were convinced the Messianic Age had begun with Jesus but the world remained unchanged and evil continued. Thus Paul speaks of "this present, evil Age" (Gal. 1:4) and "the god of this Age"—Satan (2 Cor. 4:4) and looks forward to full deliverance (Rom. 8:22) at the return of Messiah Jesus (Phil. 1:6).

297. Using Crossan's distinction between the apocalyptic rule of God and the sapiential rule of God, the Kingdom (rule) of God which has arrived is the sapiential Kingdom "which looks to the present... and imagines how one could live here and now within an already or always available divine dominion" (*loc. cit.*, p. 292). It can be considered the hidden or only partially evident reign of God. It is quite similar to 'realized eschatology.'

298. This then is the fully manifested and consummated apocalyptic Kingdom (rule) of God whose "consummation would be objectively visible and tangible to all." *Ibid.*

299. For a survey of various such expectations at the time of Jesus in the Pseudepigrapha, cf. e.g. Duling, *op.cit.*, p. 51 and J. Ford "Millenium," *Anchor Bible Dictionary* (1992), Vol. 4, p. 832. The Funk group remarks that Mk. 10:30 "could well have come from Jesus" (*op. cit.*, p. 165) but only if the details are "metaphorical." This reflects their assumption that at no point in his ministry could Jesus have anticipated a temporal glorious Kingdom on earth.

300. Cf. the extended discussion in Taylor, *op. cit.*, pp. 433-435. Cf. also Anderson, *op. cit.*, pp. 251f.

301. Cf. Crossan's "sapiential rule of God" noted earlier (notes 294 and 297 *supra*).

302. Cf. e.g. the discussion in J. Jeremias, *The Parables of Jesus* (1963), pp. 16ff. Only in this way can the variety of literary forms

designated by the word *parabolē* in the Gospels be accounted for. *Ibid.*, note 22, p. 16 and p. 20.

303. Cf. *op. cit.*, p. 439. Cf. also Jeremias, *New Testament Theology*, pp. 177f.; Funk (*Parables*, p. 65) prints it in grey.

304. Fitzmyer notes this change in Jesus: "Jesus does not continue to appear in the Gospel as the kind of 'more powerful one' that John had expected him to be—a fiery reformer." *Luke 1*, p. 477; cf. also pp. 663f.

305. So Crossan, *op. cit.*, p. 449, no. 454; Jeremias, *Parables*, p. 170; Fitzmyer, *Luke 2*, p. 1005. Funk, *Parables*, p. 60.

306. It is interesting to note that according to Charles, in the early 1st Christian century *Testament of Moses* the consummation of the Kingdom is to be preceded by a period of repentance (*op. cit.*, p. 301): "so that his name may be called upon till the day of recompence (or repentance) with regard to which the Lord will regard them in the consummation at the end of days" 1:18 as transl. by Priest in Charlesworth, *Pseudepigrapha*, p. 927, note k.

307. It has the marks of traditional material, particularly the striking reference to "in the fourth watch, in the darkest part of the watch" (v. 35). For other "primitive features" cf. Taylor, *op. cit.*, p. 182. Cf. Crossan, *op. cit.*, no. 218, p. 444. For *prōi* as the fourth watch of the night cf. Mark 13:35.

308. So also the multiply attested Q passage concerning persistent asking, seeking, knocking. Cf. Crossan, *op. cit.*, no. 4, p. 435. It is translation Greek in both Matthew (7:7-11) and Luke (11:9-13). Cf. *SC Syn G*, no. 17, pp. 92 and 95.

309. So e.g. J. Neusner, *First Century Judaism in Crisis* (1975), p. 38. Cf. also G. Vermes, *Jesus the Jew* (1981), pp. 56f. He writes: "The long and short of this argument [Pharisaic influence in Galilee] is that Pharisaic opposition to Jesus in Galilee was mostly foreign and not local" (p. 57). Cf. Martin, *Paul*, pp. 33-37. Cf. also Freyne, *op. cit.*, pp. 319ff. Cf. also Sanders, *op. cit.*, pp. 286-293.

310.   It is after 70 C.E. that the Pharisees (Rabbis) control the Synagogues. Cf. E. Smallwood, *The Jews under Roman Rule* (1981), p. 124, 133f. Cf. Martin, *ibid.*, pp. 51ff.

311.   It is not possible to determine the extent in the process of transmission to which Pharisees have artificially become part of the tradition.   In the post-70 period they are more widely represented in Galilee.

312.   This Q saying is at least doubly attested (Crossan, *op. cit.*, p. 439, no. 84) and considered by Crossan to go back to Jesus himself. *Ibid.*   It is found also in the Gospel of Thomas (cf. nos. 39 and 102); and in Pap. Oxy. 655 (*ibid.*) which was written ca 150 C.E.   Cf. B. Grenfell and A. Hunt, *New Sayings of Jesus and Fragment of a Lost Gospel* (1904), pp. 37-45; also Schweizer, *Matthew*, p. 433.

313.   Cf. Josephus' claim (*Ant.* 18:116ff.) that Herod arrested John to head off the possibility of a popular political uprising.   Cf. also Crossan's discussion, *op. cit.*, pp. 231f. and Horsley, *Bandits*, esp. pp. 247ff.

314.   Concerning these, Anderson's comments (*op. cit.*, pp. 104ff.) are significant, showing that at this time a narrow and a liberal element in Pharisaism were in dialogue/disagreement with each other over such issues.   Kümmel correctly notes that Jesus grew up in the traditions taught by the scribes and Pharisees (oral and written law) as did most Palestinian Jews at this time, but gradually comes to disagree with them on specific interpretations and emphases.   *Op. cit.*, pp. 51ff.

315.   This is his position according to v. 27, namely human beings, *as human beings*, determine appropriate Sabbath activity (taking "son of man" in verse 28 as parallel to v. 27 and equivalent to "human being" as seems most likely).   The modifications in Matthew (12:7,8) and Luke (6:5) both interpret the incident in the light of the Church's later use of "Son of Man" as a title for Jesus.

316.   It is at least triply attested by 7 different sources (So Crossan, *op. cit.*, no. 1, p. 434 and his discussion, pp. 332f.   He considers it to go back to the historical Jesus, *ibid.*, p. 434; cf. also the extended

section in Jeremias, *N.T. Theology,*, pp. 231 ff.; Fitzmyer, *Luke 2,* pp. 842ff.; Marshall, *op. cit.*, pp. 350f.). The Q account is translation Greek (*SC of Syn G,* p. 43, no. 35).

317.   Matthew recounts the death a little later (14:1ff.) and John seems to refer to John's death in 5:33-35, in close proximity to the block of material he shares independently with Mark's two traditions (Mark 6:30-7:37; Mark 8:1-26).

318.   This judgment in connection with the mission circuit is independently attested in both Mark and Q; and the Q account is translation Greek (*SC of Syn G,* no. 35, p. 43).

319.   *Op. cit.*, pp. 237ff. where   he speaks of it as a "crisis" for Jesus, resulting in a radical shift in Jesus' understanding of his mission.

320.   The fact of Herod's killing John is found also in Josephus. Cf. the discussion in n. 256.

321.   *Ibid.*

322.   John only alludes to it (5:35) and Luke radically abbreviates the notice (9:9) but in both Matthew and Mark it is detailed and both accounts are translation Greek (cf. no. 36 *SC Syn G,* p. 44).

323.   The mission tour is translation Greek in Q (cf. no. 35, *SC Syn G,* p. 43) as is the Markan account of John's death (both in the Markan and in the Matthean form. Cf. no. 36, *ibid.*, p. 44).   The miraculous feeding is translation Greek in the account preserved in Mark 8. Cf. no. 44 and no. 37 in *SC Syn G,* p. 44; cf. also, p. 31.

324.   Cf. e.g. Haenchen, *John 1*, pp. 275f.; Brown, *John 1,* pp. 236-244; and particularly the harmonized listings, pp. 238, 240-243; Martin *SC Joh*, pp. 18f.; Guelich, *op. cit.*, p. 402.

325.   While the Lukan emphasis on Jesus praying has frequently been noted, it is important to point out that this is an emphasis that came to all the Gospel writers in general from earlier traditional material.

326.   While the historicity of such a sending out of disciples (whether of 12 or 70/72) has been doubted, as Fitzmyer notes (*Luke 2*, pp. 843f.) "there is no conclusive reason to say that Jesus did not associate to himself disciples and prepare them for preaching the advent of the kingdom by sending them on this temporary mission." *Ibid.*, p. 843.   Cf. also Jeremias, *N.T. Theology*, pp. 231ff.; M. Hengel, *The Charismatic Healer and His Followers* (1981), p. 73; Sanders, *op. cit.* pp. 223f.

327.   Schweizer notes: "That Jesus restricted himself in his message exclusively to Israel (see also Mt. 15:24) is nowadays less and less a matter for dispute." *Jesus*, p. 296.   It is hard to understand why Crossan (*op. cit.*, no. 405, p. 488) considers this specific verse in Matthew (10:23) to be not from the historical Jesus, but in Stratum 3 (the period 80-120 C.E.) at which time it would obviously be irrelevant. The use of the title Son of Man might be either early or late, depending on whether it refers to Jesus or to an eschatological figure Jesus expected at the end of the Age.   Certainly in the minds of the Evangelist it would have meant Jesus himself.   It appears that Jesus held the view that only after the arrival of the New Age would the Gentiles be brought by God to join God's people.   For the variety of expectations on this matter cf. Martin, *Paul*, pp. 117ff.   Cf. also David Bosch, *Die Heidenmission in der Zukunftschau Jesu* (1959), pp. 40f. and Jeremias, *N.T. Theology*, pp. 245f.

328.   For various interpretations of this phrase cf. e.g. Taylor, *op. cit.*, pp. 385f.; Mann, *Mark*, pp. 350f.; Evans, *op. cit.*, pp. 21ff. Anderson is no doubt correct in his view that while for Mark the verse refers to the transfiguration which immediately follows in his Gospel, on the lips of Jesus, however, it would have to mean he "was predicting in the most comprehensive way the final consummation of God's purpose in the *not too distant future* (some of his hearers would live to see it)." *Op. cit.*, p. 221.   That Jesus could be mistaken in this matter should be no surprise in light of the surely authentic word of Jesus in Mark 13:32, "But of that day or that hour no one knows, not even the angels, nor the Son [i.e. Messiah], but only the Father."   Cf. Mann, *ibid.*, p. 539; Lane, *op. cit.*, p. 482. Taylor (*op. cit.*, pp. 522f.) correctly cites Schmeidel's perceptive judgment who "included the saying in his list of nine passages which he called 'the foundation pillars for a truly

scientific life of Jesus.'" Funk (*op. cit.*, p. 205) indicates "it might well be based on something Jesus actually said" but the majority of his group was "dubious that Jesus was responsible for the present wording."

329. Jeremias correctly highlights the urgency: "They are to carry out their task with utmost speed—it is the last hour..." *N.T. Theology*, p. 237; cf. also p. 160; so also Schweizer, *Jesus*, p. 296.

330. There is little doubt that the celebration of the Lord's Supper in the Church has colored the details of this narration, as well as numerous Old Testament motifs; however, the large crowd following Jesus may be an actual recollection in the tradition since it is triply attested: Mark 6:44; Mark 8:9; John 6:10— one of which (Mark 8) is translation Greek (cf. nos. 44 and 37, *SC Syn G*, p. 44).

331. *John 1*, pp. 249f.; Schweizer, *Jesus*, pp. 247f.

332. Brown considers Jn. 6:14,15 to contain "an item of correct historical information." *Ibid.* p. 249. Jeremias correctly points out that such a statement reflects the situation at the time of Jesus, not that of the early Church. *N.T. Theology*, pp. 71f.; cf. also note 2, p. 72. Cf. also the discussion in Beasley-Murray, *op. cit.*, pp. 88f. Cf., however, Haenchen, *John 1,* p. 273 and Barrett, *op. cit.*, p. 278.

333. Horsley, *Bandits*, p. 257.

334. There are a number of passages where Jesus speaks of the delay of the consummation of the Kingdom: e.g. Q passages Lk. 12:45/Mt. 24:48; Lk. 13:25/Mt. 25:5. This is explained perhaps by Lk. 13:6-9 (the barren fig tree) as providing an opportunity for repentance. Cf. also Lk. 18:8b.

335. Cf. Schweizer, *Jesus*, pp. 295, 297; O'Neill, *op. cit.*, pp. 48ff.

336. *Op. cit.*, p. 171.

337. Cf. the similar, yet quite different, form of this passage in *G. of Thomas*, no. 17. Cf. also Crossan, *op. cit.*, no. 73, p. 439.

338. Cf. the survey in C. Tuckett, "Messianic Secret," *Anchor Bible Dictionary,* Vol. 4 (1992), pp. 797ff.

339. This response of Jesus does not mean that he rejects having some special role in the Kingdom. Rather, as will be seen below, Jesus later seems to encourage by words and actions some Messianic evaluation of himself and his role and it will need to be investigated as to why this should be so.

340. Cf. Brown, *John 1*, pp. 249f., 300f. In John the cause of the defection is his offensive statement about "gnawing" his flesh and drinking his blood; this harsh language seems to be the result of Johanine editorialization of the tradition.

341. *Op. cit.*, p. 88.

342. This added material is generally ascribed to Lukan redaction of the Markan account (so, e.g. Fitzmyer, *Luke 1,* pp. 791f.). Cf. the ambivalence of Marshall, *op. cit.*, pp. 380f. The verses where Luke differs most from Mark (9:28-30, 31-33a) are translation Greek; where Luke is clearly using Mark (vv. 33b-35) he improves Mark's Greek somewhat, as is usual. Martin, *SC Syn G*, pp. 68f. and no. 50, p. 44.

343. Cf. the extended discussion in Fitzmyer, *Luke 1*, pp. 795f. where finally he concludes "Just what sort of an incident in the ministry—to which it is clearly related—it was is impossible to say." *Ibid.*, p. 796. Crossan (no. 184, p. 442) places it in his first stratum with ± indicating that in some general way it goes back to the historical Jesus (cf. *op. cit.*, p. 434).

344. Anderson correctly notes that this remark refers to the Twelve "who in their astonishment cannot comprehend that this road to Jerusalem must be God's way for Jesus" and have "a sense of impending terror." *Op. cit.*, p. 253.

345. Mark puts this immediately before the transfiguration and Luke follows him in that in spite of the viewpoint expressed in Luke's unique tradition in 9:28-33a. In any case the transfiguration experience was, no doubt, the culmination of a longer period of struggle and prayer on

the part of Jesus.

346. Schweizer aptly notes: "One would have to declare Jesus something of a simpleton if it were maintained that he went up from Galilee to Jerusalem in all innocence, without any idea of the deadly opposition he was to encounter there." *Jesus*, pp. 299ff. Similarly Crossan: "After the execution of John, and in the context of what he himself was doing, such a prophecy [of his impending death] required no transcendental information. Indeed, if the idea never crossed Jesus' mind, he was being very naive indeed," *Op. cit.*, p. 352. Cf. also Jeremias, *N. T. Theology*, pp. 286, 278-280; N. Wright, "Quest for the Historical Jesus" in *Anchor Dictionary of the Bible* (1992), Vol. 3, p. 799; Kümmel, *op. cit.*, p. 86; Fitzmyer, *Luke 2*, pp. 994, 779.

347. Cf. no. 49, in *SC Syn G*, p. 44. The subsequent two are not (cf. nos. 53 and 62, *ibid.*, p. 45). Crossan lists them in his second stratum with - (cf. no. 240, p. 444). Jeremias however, considers the second one (Mk. 9:31) as the most original. Cf. his discussion *N.T. Theology*, pp. 281f.; also Anderson, *op. cit.*, p. 232. As Jeremias has shown it is particularly significant that a number of details in the passion announcements were not fulfilled and "all this shows that these announcements of [future] suffering were by no means all formulated *ex eventu.*" *Ibid.*, pp. 284f.

348. For evidence of this common Jewish belief at the time of Jesus cf. e.g. Fitzmyer, *Luke 2*, pp. 1301f., 855; Nickelsburg, "Resurrection," pp. 685ff. It is in this sense that Jesus here speaks of his resurrection when, in God's own time, all the dead will be raised. Certainly the *later Church* would, however, have understood this tradition in terms of Jesus' unique resurrection soon after the crucifixion.

349. Cf. the discussion in Jeremias, *N.T. Theology*, pp. 278-280; 283ff. Kümmel, *op. cit.*, pp. 86-90. Jeremias notes particularly the great variety of literary forms in which Jesus expresses this awareness. *Ibid.*, pp. 282f.

350. *Ibid.*, p. 87; cf. also Fitzmyer, *Luke 2*, p. 994; Marshall, *op. cit.*, p. 545.

351. Cf. Fitzmyer, *ibid.*, p. 1032 for references.

352. The unit is translation Greek. Cf. *SC Syn G,*, p. 108, no. 39. Kümmel concludes about this passage: "Accordingly, Jesus knew that in Jerusalem he would face a fate of death, and went to Jerusalem in spite of this." *Op. cit.*, p. 86.

353. *N.T. Theology*, p. 286.

354. Cf. Kümmel, *op. cit.*, pp. 87f.; Schweizer, *Jesus*, p. 306.

355. *Ibid.* Cf. also, p. 298.

356. Cf. Sanders, *op. cit.*, p. 332; Kümmel, *op. cit.*, p. 86.

357. Cf. Fitzmyer, *Luke 2*, p. 1005; while Crossan lists it in his 3rd Stratum, he marks it + indicating it goes back to Jesus himself. *Op. cit.*, p. 449. Funk, *Parables*, p. 60 prints it in pink "Jesus probably said something like this" (*ibid.*, p. 21).

358. While Crossan puts a - by Lk. 13:34,35 though listing it in his first stratum (cf. *op. cit.*, 167, p. 442), there is no inherent reason why Jesus might not have gone to Jerusalem a number of times, since as a pious Jew he was expected to go 3 times each year. Cf. other indications in the Synoptics of more than one visit in Anderson, *op. cit.*, pp. 259f. Fitzmyer, however, (*Luke 2*, p. 1034) indicates the statement would not necessarily require that Jesus have visited Jerusalem more than once; it may only be his frequent desire for their repentance.

359. While there is a tendency to ascribe this passage to the later Church after the fall of Jerusalem (e.g. Crossan lists it in his third stratum no. 477-, p. 449), Fitzmyer after an extended discussion (*Luke 2*, pp. 1254f.) concludes: "In other words, the best solution to these problems is the recognition that the Lucan oracle may well go back to Jesus in some form..." *Ibid.*, p. 1255. It is clearly translation Greek (*SC Syn G*, no. 56, p. 108).

360. Just as in Mark 11:27-33 Jesus tells religious leaders in Jerusalem their decision to reject John = they also reject all of God's

reign, so it becomes clear to Jesus he too stands in special relation to the Kingdom and rejection of him and his message regarding the Kingdom = rejection of the Kingdom itself.

361. As will be pointed out below, Jesus does not seem to feel *he* is to bring in the Kingdom; but, rather, he waits for the Father to do so. In this way the Father vindicates Jesus' role and message.

362. *Jesus*, p. 302.

363. Sanders calls the view "'conceivable,' perhaps 'possible' that Jesus, when he knew he was going to die saw his death as that of a martyr who would be vindicated." Op. cit., p. 331. Cf. also Hengel, *Zealots*, p. 267.

364. Barrett, *op. cit.*, pp. 415f.

365. Cf. Brown, *John 1*, pp. 459-461. He concludes "that John is giving us a theological adaptation of a tradition similar to that of the Synoptics, but not the same." *Ibid.*, p. 461. Cf. also the discussion in Fitzmyer, *Luke 2,* pp. 1243f.; Martin, *SC Joh*, pp. 47, 56. Cf. the general discussion of this issue in note 36.

366. *SC Joh*, p. 46 and no. 1, p. 48.

367. So Fitzmyer, *Luke 2*, p. 1244; similarly Anderson, *op. cit.*, p. 260, though he does grant that what happened that day caused "fleeting excitement of the crowd." Whether or not this entry had anything to do with later official action on the part of the authorities is not clear, but that cannot be dismissed as an impossibility in the light of passages like Mk. 14:2; Jn. 12:9, 19 etc.

368. The translation Greek of Mark's account puts it into the earliest stage. Crossan's putting it in his 2nd Stratum (60-80 C.E.) and designating it with a sign-(=does not go back to Jesus, *op. cit.*, no. 257, p. 445) is unlikely.

369. So e.g. Sanders (*op. cit.*, p. 308): "To conclude: The entry was probably deliberately managed by Jesus to symbolize the coming of the

Kingdom and his own role in it."

370.   Matthew has changed Mark's one animal to two, misunderstanding the parallelism of the Hebrew poetry of Zech. 9:9, thus presenting the ridiculous picture of Jesus riding on both *"of them."* (Mt. 21:7)!

371.   Jesus' intention in arranging such a strange way of finding an animal and choosing to ride it while his disciples walk would be directed both at the disciples, who as shall be seen below, have a variety of ideas about Jesus and his role in the Kingdom; as well as, toward the crowds some of whom were among the many who at one time followed him in Galilee and had brought with them various expectations about Jesus.

372.   Fitzmyer, *Luke 2*, p. 1249, disagrees. It is clear, however, that while the Synoptic Gospel writers intend the instructions to show *foreknowledge*, that is a later interpretation of the strange initiative Jesus takes here.

373.   Mark only says "bystanders" (11:5); Luke changes this to "owners." There is no way to determine if the Mark phrase (omitted by Mt. and Lk.) "upon which no one has yet sat" is a part of the tradition that came to Mark or not.

374.   For a discussion of the various difficulties some find in such an interpretation of this account, cf. Marshall, *op. cit.*, pp. 709ff.

375.   Cf. e.g. Horsley, *Bandits*, pp. 37f. and 41ff.; Freyne, *op. cit.*, *passim*—particularly pp. 220, 288-291.

376.   Horsley, *ibid.*, p. 37.

377.   The extent to which these heightened expectations would have been triggered by this arrival of Jesus in Jerusalem is variously evaluated. Cf. e.g. Fitzmyer, *Luke 2*, pp. 1244f.; C. Barrett, *Jesus and the Gospel Tradition* (1967), p. 23; also *John*, p. 416. Cf. the survey in Taylor, *op. cit.*, pp. 451ff. Also the degree to which the passage from Zechariah (quoted only by Matthew and John) influenced either

Jesus' actions or Mark's account of them cannot be determined. Nor is it clear whether any in the pilgrim crowd or among Jesus' disciples would have thought of that passage. Cf. Taylor, *ibid.*, p. 451.

378. Cf. e.g. Fitzmyer, *Luke 2*, pp. 1272f.; Taylor, *op. cit.*, pp. 469f.; Marshall, *op. cit.*, pp. 723f.; Jeremias, *N.T. Theology*, pp. 55f.

379. So e.g. Anderson, *op. cit.*, p. 269; Funk, *Mark*, p. 178. Crossan puts it in his 2nd Stratum (cf. *op. cit.*, no. 261-, p. 445).

380. *Mark*, p. 457.

381. Neither of these references in Matthew and Luke are dependent on anything in Mark (who has no parallel) nor on each other.

382. Cf. Lane, *op. cit.*, p. 412; Schweizer, *Jesus*, p. 298. Cf. also Kümmel, *op. cit.*, pp. 64f.

383. It is triply attested according to Crossan and in the 1st Stratum (*op. cit.*, no. 46+, p. 437). Funk prints the Gospel of Thomas form (no. 65) in pink (cf. *Parables,* p. 51). Cf. also Jeremias, *Parables*, pp. 71ff. Fitzmyer, *Luke 2*, pp. 1277ff. While the allegorical elements in the parable are generally rejected from being authentic (with preference being given to the less allegorized Gospel of Thomas form), the story shows clear contacts with Is. 5:1ff. which is similarly allegorized (cf. v. 7). This indicates that there is no fundamental reason Jesus' Jewish *mathla* could not contain allegorical elements.

384. Matthew (20:21) has taken it this way. Even if the reference is to the Messianic banquet presided over by Jesus (cf. Luke 22:29f.), the meaning is basically the same.

385. *Mark*, p. 167. Cf. also Mann, *Mark*, p. 411; Anderson, *op. cit.*, pp. 253f. Crossan lists it in his 2nd Stratum with - (no. 254, p. 445).

386. Op. cit., p. 439.

387. This seems to be a mixture of Q and Luke's special traditions (Matthew's form has the third person here with a reference to the "Son

of man"). Cf. Fitzmeyer's analysis, *Luke 2*, pp. 1411ff. Marshall (*op. cit.*, p. 815) concludes: "Although the saying stands somewhat isolated in the teaching of Jesus, its very uniqueness and dissimilarity from the teaching of the early church favour its authenticity. Certainly it fits in with the promise of rule made by Jesus to the disciples (cf. 12:32) and forms the background to the request in Mark 10:37." Cf. also p. 817. Crossan lists it in his 1st Stratum, but with - (*op. cit.*, no. 179, p. 442).

388. Cf. *Luke 2*, pp. 1507f. and 1510.

389. Cf. J. Jeremias' detailed study in *The Eucharistic Words of Jesus* (1964), pp. 160-203. The earlier mistaken objection by Jeremias to there being an Aramaic phrase behind the Greek was corrected in later editions. Cf. pp. 193f. In addition to the Aramaic evidence cited there and in Fitzmyer, *Luke 2*, p. 1395, no. 10 should be added Daniel 2:38 (lit.): "You, it, its head of gold" where the suffixed noun "its head" is able to be in a genitive relation with "gold" not because it is in the construct case, which would be impossible due to the suffix, but because the genitive relation is expressed, as is common in Aramaic, by the particle *di*. This exactly parallels the probable Aramaic (lit.), "this, it, my blood of the covenant"—the pronoun 'it' being one way of expressing a copula idea in Aramaic, as the Daniel reference illustrates.

390. Cf. the earlier discussion.

391. Cf. Taylor, *op. cit.*, p. 452; Anderson, *op. cit.*, p. 260.

392. Kümmel notes (*op. cit.*, p. 73) "it is entirely possible that this designation [Son of David] of the political savior was occasionally used with reference to Jesus." Horsley (*Bandits*, pp. 90ff.) shows that the expectation of a nationalistic messianic royal ruler of the line of David was especially characteristic of the ordinary people (in contrast to the literate groups) in the 1st century C.E. Cf. also Horsley, "Popular," p. 487.

393. Cf. Horsley, *ibid.*, pp. 88f.; Sanders, *op. cit.*, p. 295; Merkel, *op. cit.*, p. 981; Hengel, "Charismatic," p. 39; Kümmel, *Theology*, p. 72.

394. For the view that this is a later, anachronistic usage of Luke cf.

Fitzmyer, *Luke 1,* p. 619. It is surprising if Luke would change Simon's name to one with clearly political overtones at the time of Luke unless he found it in some of his traditional material. Cf. also, Marshall, *op. cit.,* p. 240. Whether Judas Iscariot's name reflects association with the Sicarii, while possible, is considered unlikely. Cf. Fitzmyer, *ibid.,* p. 620; Marshall, *ibid.,* pp. 240f. Cf. also Jeremias, *Theology,* p. 72.

395. Cf. *SC Joh,* nos. 68, 69, p. 54.

396. Fitzmyer (*Luke 2,* p. 1554ff.) sees it largely as Lukan redaction, but, perhaps, going back to a pre-Lukan tradition from his L source with origin in the earliest period. Cf. Marshall (*op. cit.,* pp. 890f.) also.

397. So Anderson, *op. cit.,* p. 217; Taylor, *op. cit.,* p. 380; Kümmel, *op. cit.,* p. 69.

398. This is very Semitic, possibly translation Greek. Cf. no. 58 *SC Syn,* p. 109 and pp. 99-101 of *Syn Ev.* Most see it as a pre-Lukan tradition. Cf. e.g. Fitzmyer, *Luke 2,* p. 1429.

399. Cf. Fitzmyer, *ibid.;* Marshall, *op. cit.,* pp. 823ff.

400. Cf. Marshall, *ibid.,* p. 824.

401. The words "with persecutions" is, however, generally and correctly ascribed to later editing. Cf. e.g. Taylor, *op. cit.,* p. 433; Anderson, *op. cit.,* pp. 251f.

402. Cf. chap. 3, p. 34 *supra.*

403. Cf. e.g. Taylor, *op. cit.,* p. 452; cf. also Barrett, *op. cit.,* p. 416; Sanders, *op. cit.,* p. 119.

404. Cf. e.g. Kümmel, *op. cit.,* p. 73. Cf. the extended discussions in Fitzmyer, *Luke 2,* pp. 1309-1314. Taylor, *op. cit.,* pp. 490-493. Anderson, *op. cit.,* pp. 283ff.; Marshall, *op. cit.,* pp. 743-749. It is quite Semitic (cf. no. 13, p. 49, *SC Syn*). Fitzmyer points out that the pun in Ps. 110:1 was perfectly possible in Aramaic, the language Jesus "was

probably speaking." The occurrence of such a dialogue need not in itself require that Ps. 110 was generally understood Messianically by Jews at the time of Jesus. Cf. the extended discussion in Fitzmyer, *ibid.*, p. 1311; Marshall, *ibid.*, p. 748.

405. Marshall, *op. cit.*, pp. 744, 746; Anderson, *op. cit.*, p. 284.

406. Fitzmyer writes: "The real problem in understanding the episode is not the meaning it has in Stage III of the gospel tradition (what the evangelists imply by it), but what it would have meant in Stage I." *Luke 2*, pp. 1313f.

407. *Ibid.*, p. 1312. Cf. Marshall, *op. cit.*, pp. 744f. and the references listed there.

408. So e.g Anderson, *op. cit.*, p. 284; Fitzmyer, *Luke 2*, p. 1312; Taylor, *op. cit.*, p. 491; Marshall, *op. cit.*, p. 744; Brown, *Birth*, pp. 508ff.; Jeremias, *Theology*, pp. 259, 276, note 2.

409. So e.g. F. Filson, *Matthew* (1960), p. 240; Mann (*Matthew*, p. 274) says "It is in fact just as easily interpreted as deliberately casting doubt on the whole idea [of Davidic descent of the Messiah]." Kümmel writes: "this [passage] clearly says that Jesus rejected for himself the expectation of a son of David who should fulfill the political hopes." *Op. cit.*, p. 73. Cf. also Fitzmyer (*Luke 2*, p. 1312) and the supporters of this view cited there.

410. *Op. cit.*, p. 73.

411. Cf. the discussion, chap. 1 *supra.*, pp. 11ff.

412. Cf. Horsley, *Bandits*, p. 102. Cf. also Mann, *Matthew*, p. 275.

413. The Damascus Document (CD) is the Qumran form of what Charles called "Fragments of a Zadokite Work." In both the word Messiah is *singular* (cf. Frag. 2:10, CD 2:12; CD 6:1; Frag. 9:10B; Frag. 9:29B, CD 20:1; Frag. 15:4). Cf. Charles, *Pseudepigrapha*, pp. 799ff.; P. Davies, *The Damascus Covenant* (1982), pp. 232ff.

414. Cf. note 413 *supra.* The Document is dated early in the 1st century B.C.E.

415. "Fragments," p. 788.

416. the reference here is specifically to Mariamne's two sons by Herod, Alexander and Aristobolus. *Ibid.*, p. 788.

417. *Ibid.*

418. Cf. e.g his discussion *ibid.*, pp. 795f.

419. Cf. e.g. Sanders, *op. cit.* p. 332; Charles, *Eschatology*, p. 376: Jesus "at the outset of his ministry had, we can hardly doubt, hoped to witness the consummation of this kingdom without passing through the gates of death."

420. Sanders, *ibid.*; Schweizer, *Jesus*, p. 294. The death of the Messiah was expected in some Jewish speculation as the traditions reflected e.g. in 4 Ezra 7:29f. show. Mowinckel writes: " That the rule of the Messiah will one day come to an end, and be replaced by something still more glorious, is thus a familiar thought in Judaism, and the result of the conflict between the older, this-worldly eschatology and the later, other-worldly type." Op. cit., p. 327. He notes, further, "the death of the Messiah was not held to have any organic conexions with his sufferings; nor was there any question of an atoning death." *Ibid.*

421. The small private Passover meal would be in many ways an ideal time for Jesus' enemies to arrest him unobtrusively.

422. Matthew (26:17-20) removes many of these features; Luke (22:7-14) to a lesser degree.

423. Anderson (*op. cit.*, p. 310), however, reflects the judgment of many that "the form in which this story is told does *not* [italics added] encourage speculation about whether or how Jesus could have made practical arrangements in advance with the householder." Marshall (*op. cit.*, p. 789) in contrast: "The story itself suggests that Jesus made arrangements to hold the meal secretly, possibly to avoid arrest before

he had completed what he intended to do." The solution may, however, be that *in the tradition* Jesus did make secret, private arrangements; in the Gospel writers' *use* of the tradition, these features are taken as evidence of Jesus' control and foreknowledge. Cf. also Mann, *Mark*, pp. 564f.

424. Luke names them: "Peter and John" (v. 8) That would be a natural editorial addition. Later, however, Mark says Jesus came with the Twelve (v. 17) which could imply the two sent were not from the Twelve.

425. It is probable, as the traditions indicate, that Jesus knew at least one of his group was unreliable.

426. Cf. e.g. Marshall, *op. cit.*, p. 792. Also Taylor, *op. cit.*, pp. 537f.

427. This small detail may be an indication that the two sent are not automatically recognizable by the householder as Jesus' emissaries. Such relatively unknown disciples would not attract the attention of any outsiders who might be watching for some indication of Jesus' movements and plans.

428. Luke omits the pronoun.

429. It is probable that the house in Jerusalem in which the earliest Christians meet (cf. Acts 1:13; 4:31; and especially 12:12) is the one in which Jesus' last meal was eaten. This was the house of John Mark (Acts 12:12f.) and suggests the most natural understanding of the strange notice in Mark 14:51 of the young man who had followed Jesus (having dressed hastily) from the house of the last meal to Gethsemane and flees naked from the scene of the arrest.

430. Since such strange details are not common in Mark's narration of other activity, it does not seem probable he has created them here, but rather follows a tradition which came to him.

431. Cf. the discussions *re* historicity in Fitzmyer, *Luke 2,* p. 1439; Mann, *Mark*, pp. 588f.; Taylor, *op. cit.*, p. 551; Brown, *John 2,* pp.

814f.; Jeremias, *Theology,*, pp. 137f.; Kümmel, *op. cit.*, pp. 90f.

432. Cf. *SC Joh*, no. 42, p. 52. The Hebrews (5:7f.) account shows no evidence of dependence on the Synoptics.

433. Cf. Fitzmyer, *Luke 2*, p. 1438 where he cites the evidence (and some who hold this view), though he himself, finally, rejects it, seeing the Lukan account as a "stark abridgment of the Markan." Cf. the extended discussion in *SC Joh*, no. 42, p. 66.

434. Jesus "avowal of abstinence" in Mark 14:25 until he drinks wine with them in the Kingdom is a clear indication that Jesus either expects the consummation of the Kingdom or his own death to be extremely near. This verse in Mark is highly Semitized. Cf. Jeremias, *Theology*, pp. 182ff. Cf. the extended discussion in Taylor also (*op. cit.*, p. 547); also Sanders, *op. cit.*, p. 332.

435. The Johannine reference to "drinking the cup" (18:11) in response to Peter's having cut off the servant's ear in the Garden, is an independent testimony to the traditional nature of Jesus' Gethsemane prayer in Mark "Let this cup pass from me, nevertheless not what I want, but what you want" (Mk. 14:36).

436. Cf. *SC Joh,* no. 43, p. 52.

437. Cf. the preliminary statement in the Preface, *supra.*

438. *Op. cit.*, p. 594; cf. also Jeremias, *Theology*, p. 189; Mann, *Mark*, p. 650. It is, indeed, remarkable then that the Funk group prints the words in black, signifying "Jesus did not say this!" Cf. *op. cit.*, pp. 229 and xxii.

439. So Jeremias, *ibid.* Cf. the listing in Taylor (*op. cit.*, p. 594) for other supporters of this view.

440. *Ibid.* Cf. also, Filson, *op. cit.*, pp. 296f.

441. Cf. Jeremias' citation of the Targum in *Theology*, n. 2, p. 5. His view that Matthew's form which has *ēli* is the more original is

hardly correct since it is more likely that Matthew's text is an editorial alteration of Mark. The response of the crowd is more likely to be an editorial addition than is this unique Markan Aramaic; and thus the response of the crowd should not be used to justify following the texts of D, etc. and of Matt. 27:46 which have been conformed to the Targum of Ps. 22, as Lane, e.g. does *Mark*, p. 570, n. 65. Cf. also Mann, *Mark*, p. 650.

442. The Gospel of Peter (5:19) has "(my) power, power why have you deserted me?" (Cf. M. Mara, *Evangile de Pierre*, 1973, p. 48), which may be an editorial modification of the Markan form (especially without Harnack's conjectural addition of "my") to soften the apparent loss of trust in God on the part of Jesus. But cf. Crossan's differing judgment, *The Cross That Spoke*, (1988), pp. 220-224.

443. This is very much like the situation of Job who cries out again and again to God for an assurance of his presence and for an explanation of his ways (e.g. Job 13:20-24), yet never gives up his trust; who learns to trust even when he cannot understand.

444. Cf. Kümmel, *op. cit.*, pp. 94f.

445. Cf. e.g. Horsley, *Bandits*, p. 89.

446. Brown (*John 1*, p. 46) correctly notes: "It is noteworthy that, although Jesus did not claim the title of Messiah for himself and accepted the designation only with reluctance and reservations, the early Christians seized on 'Messiah' as his title par excellence and in its Greek form 'Christ' became part of his proper name."

447. Kümmel points out: "But if Jesus was condemned by Pilate as a claimant to the political rule over the Jewish people—and according to the inscription on the cross, this may be considered as certain as the fact of the crucifixion itself—then his preaching or his behavior must have given some kind of occasion for the accusation." *Ibid.*, p. 72.

448. Cf. Sanders (*op. cit.*, p. 3): "It has proved difficult to do justice to the question posed by Joseph Klausner: how was it that Jesus lived totally within Judaism, yet was the origin of a movement that

separated from Judaism..."

449. Cf. e.g. Mk. 14:50, 66ff.; 15:40-43; 16:8, 14; Mt. 28:17; Lk. 24:11, 36ff.; Jn. 20:19; Acts 1:6.

450. Five of these accounts are translation Greek: Mark's account of the empty tomb (Mk. 16:1-8—no. 61, *SC Joh,* p. 54); Luke's account of the Emmaus experience (Lk. 24:13-35—nos. 68, 69 *ibid.*); and three of John's appearance accounts: The appearance to Mary Magdalene (Jn. 20:11-18—no. 74, *ibid.*); the appearance to the disciples and Thomas (Jn. 20:24-29—no. 76, *ibid.*); Jesus' dialogue with Peter (Jn. 21:15-19—no. 79, *ibid.*).

451. Paul refers to his experience with the resurrected Jesus in a number of places in his letters (Gal. 1:11-16; 1 Cor. 9:1; 15:8-10; 2 Cor. 4:6; Phil. 3:4ff.).

452. Martin, *Early Paul,* p. 105.

453. Cf. *ibid.,* p. 108.

454. *Ibid.,* pp. 113ff.

455. Aramaic would use no copula; Greek could use one, but often omits it.

456. Cf. Arndt-Gingrich, *op. cit.,* p. 895 and the Pauline passages cited under each category there. This is especially clear in those instances when Paul writes Christ [= Messiah] Jesus.

457. Cf. Martin, *Early Paul,* pp. 238f.

458. Cf. also Martin, *Paul,* pp. 113-117.

459. The dot on this diagram and the subsequent ones indicates where the writer conceives himself to be. The similarity of the diagram of Paul's expectations and also that of Mark which follows to Jesus' final expectations concerning the consummation of the Kingdom (cf. Appendix 2, no. 6) is striking.

460. Cf. chap. II "Q Material" in *SC Syn G*, pp. 89-103.

461. Cf. "Introduction," *supra.*

462. *Op. cit.*, pp. 60-64.

463. The 17 syntactical criteria of syntax criticism are a broader spectrum of *frequent* usage than those selected by Kloppenborg.

464. The number before each section refers to the numbering of Q sections in Martin, *Syntax Criticism of the Synoptic Gospels*, pp. 90-93, 95. For Kloppenborg's classification of Q material cf. *op. cit.*, pp. viii-x.

465. Op. cit., pp. 61ff.

466. Cf. the counts and percentages at the end of this appendix.

467. For a more exact description of this feature cf. Syn Ev, pp. 19f. and p. 46.

468. For a more exact description of this feature cf. Syn Ev, pp. 21ff. and p. 46.

469. For a more exact description of this feature (which may explan the large discrepancy between Kloppenborg's counts and mine here), cf. Syn Ev, pp. 30f. and p. 47.

470. Cf. the detailed discussion of this in *Syn Ev,* pp. 40-43; *SC Syn G*, pp. 9-25; *SC Joh*, pp. 163-165.

471. For a more detailed discussion of Matthew's and Luke's treatment of Mark cf. *SC Syn G*, pp. 37-74 and pp. 127f.; for Q cf. pp. 96-98.

472. Cf. *ibid.*, p. 93.

473. Twelve are units of 4-15 lines in length; 2 are 23 lines long. Cf. *ibid.*, pp. 91-93. Cf. also *ibid.*, Charts III A and III B, pp. 21f.; also

Charts IV A, B, pp. 23f.

474. Cf. *SC Syn G*, p. 52.

475. The pages listed after the various items refer to the main body of this study. The X in the diagrams designates God's ultimate act of intervention; the . in the diagrams indicates where Jesus considers himself to be in relation to the arrival of the reign of God. The   in the later diagrams indicates the beginning of the Messianic Age as distinct from God's final act of intervention.

476. The similarity of Jesus' view here just before his death to that of Paul and Mark is striking. Cf. also the Epilogue *supra*.

Bibliography

Aland, K. *Synopsis Quattuor Evangeliorum.* 1969.

Anderson, C. *The Historical Jesus.* 1972.

Anderson, H. *The Gospel of Mark.* 1981.

_____. *Jesus and Christian Origins.* 1964.

Arndt, W. and Gingrich, F. *A Greek-English Lexicon of the New Testament.* 1957.

Avi-Jonah, M. "Aenon." *Interpreter's Dictionary of the Bible.* Vol. 1. 1962.

Barrett, C. "The Background of Mark 10:45." *New Testament Essays.* ed. by A. Higgins. 1959.

_____. *The Gospel According to St. John.* 1978.

_____. *Jesus and the Gospel Tradition.* 1967.

Beasley-Murray, G. *John. Word Biblical Commentary.* 1987.

Bell, J. *The Roots of Jesus: A Genealogical Investigation.* 1983.

Betz, O. *What Do We Know About Jesus?* 1968.

Blau, L. "Bat Kol." *Jewish Encyclopedia.* Vol. II. 1902.

Boers, H. "Review" of Kloppenborg. *Interpretation.* Vol. 43 (1989).

Boring, M. "Criteria of Authenticity." *Forum.* Vol. 1 (1985).

_____. "Review" of Kloppenborg. *Journal of American Academy of Religion.* Vol. 58(1990).

Bornkamm, G. *Jesus of Nazareth.* 1960.

Bosch, D. *Die Heidenmission in der Zukunftsschau Jesu.* 1959.

Bouquet, A. *Everyday Life in New Testament Times.* 1953.

Bowker, J. *Jesus and the Pharisees.* 1973.

Braun, H. *Jesus of Nazareth. The Man and His Time.* 1979.

Braund, D. "Archelaus." *Anchor Bible Dictionary.* Vol. 1. 1992.

Brooke, G. "Melchizedek (11 Q Melch.)." *Anchor Bible Dictionary.*

Vol. 4. 1992.

Brown, R. *The Birth of the Messiah.* 1979.

_____. "Genealogy (Christ)." *Interpreter's Dictionary of the Bible. Supplement.* 1976.

_____. *The Gospel According to John. Anchor Bible.* 2 Vols. 1966, 1970.

_____. *Jesus, God and Man.* 1967.

Brownlee, W. "John the Baptist in the New Light of Ancient Scrolls." *The Scrolls and the New Testament.* ed. by K. Stendahl. 1957.

Bruce, F. *Hard Sayings of Jesus.* 1983.

Bultmann, R. *The Gospel of John.* 1971.

_____. *Jesus and the Word.* 1958.

Caird, G. "Chronology of the N.T." *Interpreter's Dictionary of the Bible.* Vol. 1. 1962.

Cameron, R. "Thomas, Gospel of." *Anchor Bible Dictionary.* Vol. 4. 1992.

Charles, R. H. *Eschatology.* 1970.

_____, ed. *The Pseudepigrapha of the Old Testament.* 1973.

Charlesworth, J., ed. *Jesus' Jewishness.* 1991.

_____. *Jesus within Judaism.* 1988.

_____. "Research on the Historical Jesus." *Proceedings of the Irish Biblical Association.* No. 9. 1985.

_____. "Review" of E. P. Sanders, *Jesus and Judaism. Journal of the American Academy of Religion.* Vol. 55 (1987).

_____, ed. *The Old Testament Pseudepigrapha.* Vol. 1. 1983.

Chilton, B. "Review" of E. P. Sanders, *Jesus and Judaism. Journal of Biblical Literature.* Vol. 106 (1987).

Clark, K. "Bethany." *Interpreter's Bible Dictionary.* Vol. 1. 1962.

Collins, A. "Review" of J. Kloppenborg. *Catholic Biblical Quarterly.* Vol. 50 (1988).

Collins, J. "Essenes." *Anchor Bible Dictionary.* Vol. 2. 1992.

Conzelmann, H. *Acts of the Apostles. Hermeneia.* 1987.

Cooke, G. *Ezekiel. International Critical Commentary.* 1951.

Crossan, J. *The Cross That Spoke.* 1988.

_____. *Four Other Gospels.* 1985.

_____. *The Historical Jesus.* 1991.

Dahl, N. *The Crucified Messiah and Other Essays.* 1974.

Daniel-Ropes, H. *Daily Life in Palestine at the Time of Christ.* 1962.

Davies, P. *The Damascus Covenant.* 1982.

De Jonge, M. "Messiah." *Anchor Bible Dictionary.* Vol. 4. 1992.

De Vaux, R. *Archeology and the Dead Sea Scrolls.* 1973.

Dibelius, M. *Jesus.* 1963.

Dodd, C. *The Founder of Christianity.* 1970.

_____. *Historical Tradition in the Fourth Gospel.* 1963.

Donfried, K. "Chronology, New Testament." *Anchor Bible Dictionary.* Vol. 1. 1992.

Duling, D. "Kingdom of God, Kingdom of Heaven." *Anchor Bible Dictionary.* Vol. 4. 1992.

Eppstein, V. "The Historicity of the Gospel Account of the Cleansing of the Temple." *Zeitschrift für die Neutestamentliche Wissenschaft.* Vol. 55 (1964).

Evans, O. "Kingdom of God." *Interpreter's Dictionary of the Bible.* Vol. 3. 1962.

Falk, H. *Jesus the Pharisee.* 1985.

Filson, F. *A New Testament History.* 1964.

_____. *St. Matthew.* 1960.

Finch, R. *The Synagogue Lectionary and the New Testament.* 1939.

Fitzmyer, J. *The Gospel According to Luke. Anchor Bible.* 2 Vols. 1981.

_____. "The Priority of Mark and the Q Source in Luke." *Jesus and Man's Hope.* 1970.

_____. *A Wandering Aramean.* 1979.

Flemington, W. "Baptism." *Interpreter's Dictionary of the Bible.* Vol. 1. 1962.

Flusser, D. *Jesus.* 1969.

_____. *Die rabbinischen Gleichnisse und der Gleichniserzählen Jesu.* 1981.

Ford, J. "Millenium." *Anchor Bible Dictionary.* Vol. 4. 1992.

Fortna, R. *The Fourth Gospel and Its Predecessor.* 1988.

_____. *The Gospel of Signs.* 1970.

Fotheringham, J. "The Evidence of Astronomy and Technical Chronology for the Date of the Crucifixion." *Journal of Theological Studies.* Vol. 35 (1984).

Freyne, S. *Galilee: from Alexander the Great to Hadrian* (323 B.C.E. to 135 C.E.). 1980.

Friedrich, G. "EUAGGELIZOMAI." *Theological Dictionary of the New Testament.* Vol. 2. 1971.

Funk, R. *et al. The Gospel of Mark (Red Letter Edition).* 1991.

_____. *The Parables of Jesus (Red Letter Edition).* 1988.

Grenfell, B. and Hunt, A. *New Sayings of Jesus and Fragments of a Lost Gospel from Oxyrhynchus.* 1904.

Gingrich, F. "Heli." *Interpreter's Dictionary of the Bible.* Vol. 2. 1962.

Grant, M. *Jesus: An Historian's Review of the Gospels.* 1977.

Guelich, R. *Mark. Word Biblical Commentary.* Vol. 34A. 1989.

Guilding, A. *The Fourth Gospel and Jewish Worship.* 1960.

Haenchen, E. *John. Hermeneia.* 2 Vols. 1984.

_____. *Acts of the Apostles.* 1971.

Harvey, A. *Jesus and the Constraints of History.* 1982.

Hengel, M. *Between Jesus and Paul.* 1983.

_____. *The Charismatic Healer and His Followers.* 1981.

_____. "PHATNE." *Theological Dictionary of the New Testament.* Vol. 9. 1974.

_____. *Zealots.* 1989.

Higgins, A. *The Son of Man in the Teachings of Jesus.* 1980.

Hodgson, R. "Review" of Kloppenborg. *Biblica.* Vol. 70. 1989.

Holladay, J. "House, Israelite." *Anchor Bible Dictionary.* Vol. 3. 1992.

Hollenbach, P. "The Conversion of Jesus: From Jesus the Baptizer to Jesus the Healer." *Aufstieg und Niedergang der Römischen Welt.*

Horsley, R. and Hanson, J. *Bandits, Prophets and Messiahs.* 1985.

_____ "Messianic Movements in Judaism." *Anchor Bible Dictionary.* Vol. 4. 1992.

_____. "Popular Messianic Movements." *Catholic Biblical Quarterly.* Vol. 46 (1984).

Howard, D. "Nathan." *Anchor Bible Dictionary.* Vol. 4. 1992.

Howard, V. "Did Jesus Speak of His Own Death?" *Catholic Biblical Quarterly.* Vol. 39 (1977).

Jackobson, A. "Review" of Kloppenborg. *Journal of Biblical Literature.* Vol. 105 (1989).

Jaubert, A. *The Date of the Last Supper.* 1965.

Jenni, E. "Messiah, Jewish." *Interpreter's Dictionary of the Bible.* Vol. 3. 1962.

Jeremias, J. *The Eucharistic Words of Jesus.* 1964.

_____. *Jesus' Promise to the Nations.* 1958.

_____. *The Parables of Jesus.* 1963.

_____. *New Testament Theology.* 1971.

_____. "Patriarchs, Testament of the Twelve." *Anchor Bible Dictionary*. Vol. 5. 1992.

_____. "XRIW." *Theological Dictionary of the New Testament*. Vol. 9. 1974.

Juel, D. *Messiah and Temple*. 1977.

Kee, H. *Jesus in History*. 1971.

Kloppenborg, J. *The Formation of Q*. 1987.

_____. *Q Parallels*. 1988.

_____. *Q-Thomas Reader*. 1990.

Koester, H. *Ancient Christian Gospels*. 1990.

_____. *History and Literature of Early Christianity*. Vol. 2. 1982.

Kraeling, K. *John the Baptist*. 1951.

Kümmel, W. *The Theology of the New Testament*. 1973.

Lane, W. *The Gospel According to Mark*. 1974.

Leaney, R. "The Birth Narratives in St. Luke and St. Matthew." *New Testament Studies*. Vol. 8 (1961-62).

Mann, C. "The Historicity of the Birth Narratives." *Chronology in the NewTestament*. ed. by Nineham. 1965.

_____. *Matthew. Anchor Bible*. 1971.

_____. *Mark. Anchor Bible*. 1986.

Manson, T. *The Servant Messiah*. 1980.

Marshall, I. *The Gospel of Luke*. 1979.

Martin, Raymond. "The Date of the Cleansing of the Temple in John 2:13-22." *Indian Journal of Theology*. Vol. 15 (1966).

_____. *Studies in the Life and Ministry of the Early Paul and Related Issues*. 1993.

_____. *Syntactical Evidence of Semitic Sources in Greek Documents (Syn Ev)*. 1974.

_____. *Syntax Criticism of Johannine Literature, the Catholic Epistles and the Gospel Passion Accounts (SC Joh)*. 1989.

_____. *Syntax Criticism of the Synoptic Gospels (SC Syn)*. 1987.

Martin-Achard, R. "Resurrection (OT)." *Anchor Bible Dictionary*. Vol. 5. 1992.

McArthur, H. *In Search of the Historical Jesus*. 1970.

McKelvey, R. *The New Temple*. 1969.

Meier, J. "Reflections on Jesus-of-History Search Today." *Jesus' Jewishness*. ed. by J. Charlesworth. 1991.

Menard, J. "Thomas, Gospel of." *Interpreter's Dictionary of the Bible. Supplement*. 1976.

Merkel, H.   "Zealot."   *Interpreter's Dictionary of the Bible. Supplement.* 1976.

Meyer, B. *The Aims of Jesus.* 1979.

_____. "Jesus Christ." *Anchor Bible Dictionary.* Vol. 3. 1992.

Meyers. E. and Strange, F.   *Archeology, the Rabbis and Early Christianity.* 1981.

Mowinckel, S. *He That Cometh.* 1959.

Murphy-O'Connor, J. "Qumran, Khirbet." *Anchor Bible Dictionary.* Vol. 5. 1992.

Neirynck, F. *Q-Synopsis.* 1988.

Neusner, J. *First Century Judaism in Crisis.* 1975.

_____. *Judaism in the Beginning of Christianity.* 1984.

Nickelsburg, G. "Resurrection (Early Judaism and Christianity)." *Anchor Bible Dictionary.* Vol. 5. 1992.

Ogg, G. *The Chronology of the Public Ministry of Jesus.* 1940.

Oliver, H. "The Lukan Birth Stories." *New Testament Studies.* Vol. 10 (1963-64).

O'Neill, J. *Messiah.* 1980.

Perrin, N. *Rediscovering the Teaching of Jesus.* 1967.

Reisner, R. "Essene Gate." *Anchor Bible Dictionary.* Vol. 2. 1992.

Robinson, J. "The Baptism of John and the Qumran Community." *Harvard Theological Review.* Vol. 50 (1957).

Ropes, J. *The Epistle of St. James.* 1916.

Sanders, E. P. *Jesus and Judaism.* 1985.

_____. *Jesus, the Gospels and the Church.* 1987.

Sandmel, S. "Archelaus." *Interpreter's Dictionary of the Bible.* Vol. 1. 1962.

Schillebeeckx, E. *Jesus.* 1979.

Schneider, J. "ERCOMAI." *Theological Dictionary of the New Testament.* Vol. 2. 1971.

Schoeps, H. *Paul.* 1961.

Schweizer, E. "Eine Hebraisierende Sonderquelle des Lukas?" *Theologische Literaturzeitung.* Vol. 6 (1950).

_____. *The Good News According to Matthew.* 1977.

_____. *The Good News According to Mark.* 1970.

_____. *Jesus.* 1971.

Silver, H. *A History of Messianic Speculation in Israel.* 1972.

Smallwood, E. *The Jews under Roman Rule.* 1981.

Smith, M.   *Clement of Alexandria and the Secret Gospel of Mark.*

1973.

Sparks, H. "The Semitisms of Acts." *Journal of Theological Studies.* n.s. Vol. 1 (1950).

_____. "The Semitisms of St. Luke's Gospel." Vol. 44 (1943).

Stauffer, E. *Jesus and His Story.* 1960.

Stein, R. "The 'Criteria' for Authenticity." *Gospel Perspectives.* Vol. 1 (1980).

Stroker, W. "Extracanonical Parables and the Historical Jesus." *The Historical Jesus and the Rejected Gospels.* ed. by C. Hedrick. 1988.

Sziksai, S. "Nathan." *Interpreter's Dictionary of the Bible.* Vol. 3. 1962.

Tatum, W. *In Quest of Jesus.* 1982.

Taylor, V. *The Gospel According to St. Mark.* 1981.

Throckmorton, B. "Genealogy (Christ)." *Interpreter's Dictionary of the Bible.* Vol. 2. 1962.

Tuckett, C. "Messianic Secret." *Anchor Bible Dictionary.* Vol. 4. 1992.

_____. "Q (Gospel Source)." *Anchor Bible Dictionary.* Vol. 5. 1992.

Turner, N. "The Relation of Luke I and II to Hebraic Sources and to the Rest of Luke-Acts." *New Testament Studies.* Vol. 2 (1955-56).

Van der Woude, A. "XRIW." *Theological Dictionary of the New Testament.* Vol. 9. 1974.

Vermes, G. "Dead Sea Scrolls." *Interpreter's Dictionary of the Bible. Supplement.* 1976.

_____. *Jesus and the World of Judaism.* 1983.

_____. *Jesus the Jew.* 1981.

Wilkinson, J. *Jerusalem as Jesus Knew It.* 1982.

Winter, P. "The Main Literary Problem of the Lukan Infancy Story." *Anglican Theological Review.* Vol. 40 (1958).

_____. "Two Notes on Luke I, II with Regard to the Theory of Imitation Hebraisms." *Studia Theologica.* Vol. 7 (1953).

Wright, N. "Jesus Christ: Quest for the Historical Jesus." *Anchor Bible Dictionary.* Vol. 3. 1992.

Ziesler, J. *The Jesus Question.* 1980.

Index

Note: Pages are referred to by number alone; notes are preceded by n.

1. AUTHORS

231ff., 256f., 285, 300, 307,
327, 377f., 391, 397, 401,
403f., 426, 431, 439
Throckmorton, B. n. 81f.
Tuckett, C. nn. 37, 335
Turner, N. nn. 14, 57

Van der Woude, A. n. 142
Vermes, G. nn. 125, 132, 139,
143, 309
Winter, P. nn. 15, 21
Wright, N. n. 346

2. Biblical Citations